THE FUTURE MILLIONAIRE MINDSET

SMART FINANCIAL CHOICES FOR TEENS

CHELETA BUDDO-GAYLE

THE FUTURE MILLIONAIRE MINDSET: SMART FINANCIAL CHOICES FOR TEENS.

CHRIST RepresentHER

ISBN: 978-969-8092-53-5 (HARDBACK)
ISBN: 978-976-97476-7-8 (PAPERBACK)
ISBN: 978-976-97476-6-1 (EBOOK)

Library of Congress Control Number: 2025924828

Scripture quotations marked (KJV) are taken from the Holy Bible, King James Version, KJV. Public domain.

Printed in the United States of America.

For inquiries, permissions, or bulk orders, contact:
Christ RepresentHER Limited
Email: christrepresenther@gmail.com

THIS BOOK BELONGS TO
THE FUTURE MILLIONAIRE:

Dedicated to my children, Czenzi and Kyrie—you are my greatest inspiration. May you both always walk boldly in purpose, knowing that you have everything inside of you to succeed.

Love,

Mom ♡

TABLE OF CONTENTS

ACKNOWLEDGMENTS

First, I give all glory and honor to God, my ultimate Provider and Source. It is by His wisdom, grace, and favor that this book exists. May it empower and equip future generations to walk in financial freedom and purpose.

To my parents, thank you for always encouraging me to be an entrepreneur. Your guidance, wisdom, and belief in me shaped my mindset and gave me the confidence to pursue financial independence from a young age.

To my husband, who has supported and inspired me on this journey—your words of encouragement, prayers, and unwavering belief in my vision mean more than I can express.

To my editors, thank you for your keen eye, dedication, and patience while refining this book. Your expertise and attention to detail have helped shape this work into something truly impactful. I appreciate your commitment to excellence and your role in making this book the best it can be.

To every future millionaire reading this book, thank you for investing in yourself. May you apply these lessons and build a future that reflects the greatness within you.

Blessings,

Cheleta Buddo-Gayle

INTRODUCTION

Imagine two roads ahead of you—one on the right and one on the left. The road on the right is rough, bumpy, and full of potholes. The road on the left is smooth, easy, and free of obstacles. Now, let me ask you: which road would you take?

Next question—do you want to be a millionaire?

Here's the truth: The road on the right is the road to becoming a millionaire—rough, unpredictable, and full of challenges. The road on the left is the road to poverty—smooth and easy, but leading nowhere. Think about my question again. Which road are you willing to take?

If, at first, you chose the smooth road and then switched to the rough road, that's great—you're already learning to adapt and embrace change.

That's exactly why I wrote this book, **The Future Millionaire Mindset: Smart Financial Choices for Teens.**

My name is Cheleta Buddo-Gayle, and I wasn't always financially savvy.

I made poor financial decisions, struggled to manage my business, and faced failure multiple times.

Today, I own and operate The Refill Store by CBC Beverages, a company specializing in purified and alkaline water production, sales of machinery and equipment for water refill stores, and consultation on setting up and operating water businesses. But before I found success, I failed—many times.

And you know what? Failing wasn't a bad thing. Because I chose to learn from my mistakes instead of being defeated by them.

I officially started my beverage manufacturing company, CBC Beverages, in August 2014. We manufactured and distributed Fruity Star (juices and drinks), along with other products like lime juice, vinegar, syrups, fruit wines, and my prized product—Pure Crystal purified water.

For years, I was trapped in financial struggles—making poor financial decisions, setting unclear goals, and surrounding myself with the wrong people.

Growing up, my parents were business owners, and they always taught me that I should own my own business too—not just work for someone else. That mindset shaped my ambition.

I knew how to make a profit, but I didn't know how to manage money—and that's where my problems began.

WHY FINANCIAL LITERACY MATTERS FOR YOUNG PEOPLE

Imagine waking up one day with the freedom to do what you love, travel where you want, bless others abundantly, and never worry about money again. Sounds like a dream, right? Well, it doesn't have to stay that way. Financial freedom is not just for a select few—it's for anyone willing to learn, make smart choices, and take consistent action.

The truth is, many adults struggle financially not because they don't earn enough, but because they were never taught how to manage their money. They live paycheck to paycheck, drowning in debt, and never experience true financial peace. But what if you could break that cycle before it even begins? What if you could start making wealth-building decisions now—before you step into adulthood?

Most people don't think about financial success until they're much older, but by then, they've often made costly mistakes. If you start now, while you're still young, you'll be miles ahead. You have the power to set yourself up for a life of financial abundance and purpose. That's what this book is all about—equipping you with the tools, wisdom, and confidence to build wealth early in life.

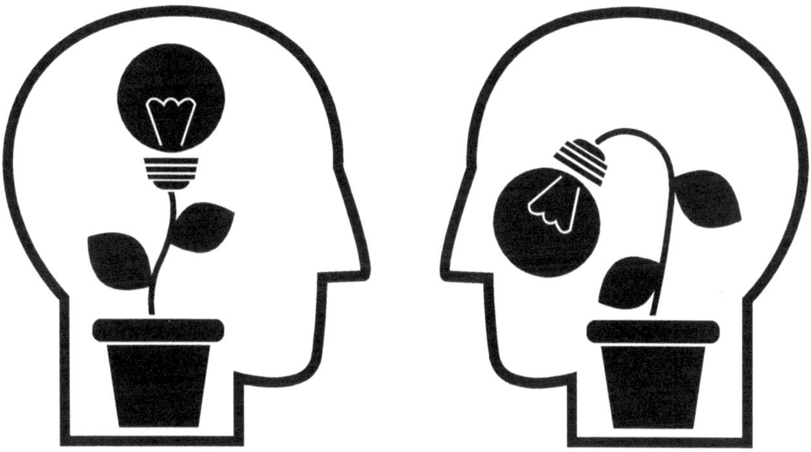

THE MILLIONAIRE MINDSET VS. THE POVERTY MINDSET

The first step to financial success is not about how much money you make—it's about how you think. There's a reason why some people seem to attract wealth effortlessly while others struggle no matter how hard they work. It all comes down to mindset.

Let's look at the difference between a Millionaire Mindset and a Poverty Mindset:

MILLIONAIRE MINDSET:

- Sees money as a tool to create opportunities and bless others
- Thinks long-term instead of chasing quick money
- Looks for solutions instead of making excuses
- Learns and grows instead of blaming circumstances
- Is generous because they understand the principle of sowing and reaping

POVERTY MINDSET:

- Sees money as scarce and constantly fears losing it
- Thinks short-term and spends impulsively
- Dwells on limitations and constantly complains about what's lacking
- Fears taking risks and avoids learning about money
- Holds onto money tightly and struggles with generosity

If you believe you'll always be broke, struggling, or just "getting by," that's likely what will happen. But if you believe you can create wealth, be a good steward, and use money wisely, you will start to attract and manage wealth in ways you never imagined.

INVESTING IN YOURSELF: THE BEST INVESTMENT YOU'LL EVER MAKE

The richest people in the world aren't just wealthy because they worked hard—they made a commitment to learn about money and build valuable skills.

The greatest investment you will ever make isn't in stocks, real estate, or a business—it's in yourself.

Here's how you can invest in yourself starting today:

Learn Financial Literacy – Money doesn't come with a guidebook, but you can read books, listen to podcasts, and take financial literacy courses to understand how it works. The more you know, the smarter your financial choices will be.

Develop High-Income Skills – Whether it's public speaking, marketing, coding, writing, or business strategy, learning valuable skills will increase your earning potential and open doors to greater financial opportunities.

Surround Yourself with Smart Mentors – Seek advice from financially wise people—whether it's a teacher, a successful entrepreneur, or a mentor who can help you level up.

Take Action on What You Learn – Knowledge alone won't make you wealthy—applying what you learn will. Every day, take one small step toward your financial goals.

Your greatest asset is YOU. When you invest in knowledge, skills, and discipline, financial success will naturally follow!

BIBLICAL PRINCIPLES OF FINANCIAL WISDOM

The Bible has over 2,300 verses about money, wealth, and stewardship—more than any other topic! That's because God cares about how we handle money. He wants us to be wise, faithful, and responsible financially.

Here are three powerful biblical principles that will guide you in building wealth:

1. Stewardship Over Ownership – **Psalm 24:1 (KJV)** says, ***"The earth is the Lord's, and the fulness thereof; the world, and they that dwell therein."*** Everything we have belongs to God, and we are simply managers of His resources. When we handle money wisely, we honor Him.

2. The Power of Diligence – **Proverbs 10:4 (KJV)** says, ***"He becometh poor that dealeth with a slack hand: but the hand of the diligent maketh rich."*** Hard work, discipline, and wise decision-making lead to prosperity.

3. The Law of Sowing and Reaping – **Galatians 6:7 (KJV)** reminds us, ***"For whatsoever a man soweth, that shall he also reap."*** We set ourselves up for future blessings when we give generously, invest wisely, and make sound financial choices.

WHAT YOU'LL LEARN IN THIS BOOK

This book isn't just about making money—it's about developing a millionaire mindset that will set you up for success in every area of life. You'll learn:

- How to earn and manage money wisely from an early age
- The best ways to save and invest for long-term financial success
- How to avoid debt and make smart spending choices
- The importance of giving and financial generosity
- Practical steps to build wealth and financial freedom before adulthood

By the time you finish this book, you'll have the knowledge and confidence to take control of your financial future. Whether you're in high school, college, or just starting out in life, the principles inside these pages will give you a head start.

Success doesn't happen overnight—it's built through consistent actions and reflections. While this book provides practical steps to develop financial habits and a business plan, journaling is a great way to track your progress, lessons, and growth.

I encourage you to use a separate journal to:

- Write down your thoughts, ideas, and business goals.
- Track your financial progress and habits.
- Reflect on challenges, wins, and lessons learned.

Your financial journey is unique to you, and keeping a journal will help you stay accountable and motivated as you apply the principles from this book! Your journey to becoming a future millionaire starts NOW. Are you ready?

LET'S GO!

TEST YOUR MILLIONAIRE MINDSET: ARE YOU READY FOR FINANCIAL SUCCESS?

Testing your knowledge is one of the best ways to make sure you truly understand and remember what you've learned. At the end of each chapter, you'll find a quick quiz to challenge yourself and reinforce key financial principles.

These quizzes aren't about getting every answer right—they're about helping you think smarter about money, business, and success.

HOW TO USE THESE QUIZZES:

- **Answer each question based on what you've learned.**
- **If you're unsure about an answer, go back and review the chapter.**
- **Check the Answer Key at the back of the book to see how well you did.**
- **Take notes on anything you need to understand better.**

The goal isn't perfection; it's progress. The more you practice, the more confident you'll become in making smart financial choices.

Ready to put your millionaire mindset to the test?

The secret to getting ahead is getting started.

MARK TWAIN

CHAPTER 1

THE MILLIONAIRE MINDSET STARTS EARLY

1. THE MILLIONAIRE MINDSET STARTS EARLY

THE POWER OF STARTING YOUNG

At just nine years old, I was already an entrepreneur. I didn't wait for someone to hand me an opportunity; I created one. While other kids were focused on playing, I was selling coloring books, crayons, regular pens, and gel ink pens to my classmates. I had the mindset of a future millionaire before I even knew what that meant.

My parents never told me to "just focus on getting a good job." Instead, they encouraged me to start my own business and think beyond the traditional 9-to-5 mindset. They planted the seed that financial freedom could be achieved through ownership and creativity.

While I didn't have all the answers back then, their guidance shaped my perspective on money and success.

But here's the truth: Having the right mindset isn't enough. Even though I was ambitious and determined to succeed, I lacked structure. I didn't have a plan, a system, or a solid strategy to sustain my business. As a result, I failed—more than once.

That's a lesson every future millionaire needs to understand. Mindset is the foundation, but structure is what builds lasting success.

WHAT IS A MILLIONAIRE MINDSET?

A millionaire mindset isn't just about wanting to be rich; it's about developing the habits, discipline, and strategies that lead to wealth.

It's about thinking ahead, making smart choices, and preparing for opportunities before they arise.

PEOPLE WITH A MILLIONAIRE MINDSET:

- See challenges as opportunities instead of roadblocks.
- Focus on learning and growth instead of making excuses.
- Plan for the long-term instead of chasing quick money.
- Understand that failure is part of the process —not the end of the road.

On the other hand, people with a **poverty mindset** believe that success is only for "lucky" people. They complain about their circumstances, avoid risks, and stay stuck in fear.

Proverbs 23:7 (KJV) says, ***"For as he thinketh in his heart, so is he..."*** What you believe about money and success will shape your reality.

If you think like a millionaire, you'll make decisions that lead to financial growth. If you think like someone who will always struggle, that's exactly what will happen.

SMART GOALS: A SIMPLE FORMULA FOR SUCCESS

When setting financial goals, it's important to be specific about what you want to achieve. The SMART goal-setting method helps you create clear and realistic goals that you can actually accomplish.

SMART

S – SPECIFIC:

What exactly do you want to achieve? (Example: I want to save $500 for a laptop.)

M – MEASURABLE:

How will you track your progress? (Example: I will save $50 per month for 10 months.)

A – ACHIEVABLE:

Is this goal realistic? (Example: I can save money by cutting back on eating out and doing side hustles.)

R – RELEVANT:

Does this goal align with your bigger plans? (Example: A laptop will help me start my online business.)

T – TIME-BOUND:

What's your deadline? (Example: I will reach this goal in 10 months.)

Now, set one SMART financial goal for yourself! Write it down and start working toward it.

LESSONS FROM MY FIRST BUSINESS FAILURE

Looking back at my little coloring book business, I realize that my biggest mistake was a lack of structure. I had a great idea, but I didn't track my sales, plan for inventory, or reinvest my money wisely. Even though I was making money, I wasn't growing my business the right way.

That's why so many people fail—not because they aren't smart or talented, but because they don't have a plan.

They earn money but don't know how to manage it. They start businesses but lack a strategy to scale. But here's the good news: You can learn from my mistakes.

HERE ARE THREE KEY LESSONS I WISH I HAD KNOWN EARLIER:

1. Track Your Money –

If you don't know where your money is going, you can't grow it. Whether you're selling snacks, styling hair, or working a part-time job, keep track of every dollar that comes in and goes out.

2. Have a Plan –

A business without a plan is just a hobby. If you want to earn real money, set clear goals, create a budget, and plan for the long term.

3. Failure is a Lesson, Not the End –

Every successful millionaire has failed at something. What separates them from others is that they learn from it and keep going.

YOUR MILLIONAIRE MINDSET STARTS NOW

You don't have to wait until you're an adult to start thinking and acting like a millionaire. The choices you make today will shape your financial future.

- Will you be a spender or a builder?
- Will you waste opportunities or create them?
- Will you let failure stop you or push you forward?

The decision is yours. If you start building the right mindset now, your future self will thank you.

QUIZ!

CHAPTER 1 QUIZ: THE MILLIONAIRE MINDSET STARTS EARLY

1. What kind of business did the author start at age 9?

A) Selling snacks
B) Selling coloring books and pens
C) Babysitting
D) Dog walking

2. What key lesson did the author learn from her first business failure?

A) Always lower your prices
B) Focus only on profits
C) Structure and planning are essential
D) Never trust customers

3. Which of the following is NOT part of a millionaire mindset?

A) Seeing challenges as opportunities
B) Blaming others for failure
C) Thinking long-term
D) Being generous

4. What Bible verse is used to support the power of mindset?

A) Matthew 6:33
B) Proverbs 23:7
C) Galatians 6:7
D) Psalm 24:1

5. What does the "S" in SMART goals stand for?

A) Spending
B) Specific
C) Saving
D) Strategy

6. What kind of mindset believes success is only for "lucky" people?

A) Growth mindset
B) Millionaire mindset
C) Poverty mindset
D) Generous mindset

7. True or False: A business without a plan is just a hobby.

A) True
B) False

8. According to the author, mindset is the ________, but structure builds success.

A) Goal
B) Shortcut
C) Foundation
D) Limitation

9. What is the first thing you should do with your money according to the SMART goals lesson?

A) Spend it
B) Lend it
C) Save or invest a portion
D) Give it away

10. Which of the following is a question you should ask yourself when setting goals?

A) Can I copy someone else's strategy?
B) Will this goal impress my friends?
C) Is this goal achievable and relevant?
D) Will this make me rich tomorrow?

"Opportunity is missed by most people because it is dressed in overalls and looks like work."

THOMAS EDISON

CHAPTER 2

EARNING YOUR FIRST DOLLAR

2. EARNING YOUR FIRST DOLLAR

THE FIRST STEP TO WEALTH: TAKING INITIATIVE

Most people believe that wealth begins with a big break, an inheritance, or a high-paying job. But in reality, financial success starts with something much simpler: earning your first dollar.

That first dollar, whether made by selling a product, offering a service, or working a small job, is the foundation of something bigger. It's not about the amount—it's about proving to yourself that you can create income. It's about breaking the mindset that says, "I have to wait for someone to give me money," and replacing it with, "I can make money happen."

No matter your age, background, or current financial situation, you have the power to create wealth from scratch. The question is: Are you willing to start?

OPPORTUNITIES ARE EVERYWHERE—IF YOU'RE WILLING TO SEE THEM

Many young people assume that without a "real job," they can't make money. But that's simply not true. Opportunities are all around; you just have to be willing to recognize and seize them.

Think about it:

- Someone out there needs help with tutoring.
- A busy person needs their car washed.
- Parents need reliable childcare.
- People are looking for handmade products, digital designs, or personal services.
- Businesses need help with social media, content creation, or errands.

The key is to stop waiting and start offering solutions.

If you start seeing problems as business opportunities, you'll never be broke another day in your life.

MY FIRST BUSINESS: THE HUSTLE MINDSET

When I started selling coloring books, crayons, and pens in prep school, I didn't have a "business strategy." I just knew that kids at my school needed these items, and I could be the one to sell them.

I didn't sit around hoping money would come to me. I went out, found a need, and filled it. That's how business works. Every millionaire you see today started with a small idea and a willingness to act.

But here's what I learned: Making money is one thing—managing it is another.

Many young entrepreneurs start small businesses but spend everything they earn instead of reinvesting it. They see money coming in, and before they know it, it's gone.

That's what happened to me. I didn't know how to manage or grow my money, so my little business eventually failed.

HOW TO START EARNING YOUR OWN MONEY

If you want to be financially independent, you need to know how to create income.

Here are three simple steps to start earning your first dollar:

1. Find a Need and Fill It –

Look for something people struggle with or need help with, then offer a solution. Whether it's selling products, offering a service, or using a skill, the key is to solve problems.

2. Start Small, But Start Now –

Don't wait for a perfect business plan. Start where you are with what you have. Sell something. Offer a service. Take action.

3. Manage Your Money Wisely –

Don't spend all your earnings. Save, reinvest, and build. The sooner you develop good financial habits, the faster you'll grow your wealth.

YOUR FINANCIAL JOURNEY BEGINS TODAY

The difference between those who succeed financially and those who struggle isn't luck—it's action.

- Some people wait for opportunities. Millionaires create them.
- Some people complain about their financial situation. Millionaires change theirs.
- Some people waste their early years. Millionaires use them to build wealth.

It's not about how much money you make—it's about learning how to think, create, and grow. If you can start small today, your future will be limitless.

Are you ready to take your first step toward financial freedom? It all begins with that first dollar.

QUIZ!

CHAPTER 2 QUIZ: EARNING YOUR FIRST DOLLAR

1. What is the main purpose of earning your first dollar?

A) To buy whatever you want
B) To prove you can make money happen
C) To start saving for retirement
D) To ask others for more money

2. True or False: You need a high-paying job to start building wealth.

A) True
B) False

3. Which mindset is being replaced when you earn your first dollar?

A) "Money grows on trees."
B) "I have to wait for someone to give me money."
C) "I am already rich."
D) "Money isn't important."

5. Which of the following is NOT mentioned as a way teens can earn money?

A) Babysitting
B) Selling handmade products
C) Becoming a doctor
D) Helping with social media

6. What did the author learn from her first business experience?

A) Selling art is the best business
B) Marketing is overrated
C) Making money is different from managing money
D) Saving is not important

7. What is Step 1 in earning your first dollar?

A) Spend what you have
B) Ask your parents for money
C) Find a need and fill it
D) Open a credit card

8. True or False: A perfect business plan is required to get started.

A) True
B) False

9. Why do many young entrepreneurs fail, according to the author?

A) They don't charge enough
B) They spend all their earnings
C) Their ideas aren't good enough
D) They work too hard

10. According to the chapter, what's the real difference between those who succeed and those who don't?

A) Intelligence
B) Money
C) Luck
D) Action

MULTIPLE
STREAMS OF
INCOME
THE SECRET
TO FINANCIAL
SECURITY

MULTIPLE STREAMS OF INCOME: THE SECRET TO FINANCIAL SECURITY

The wealthy don't rely on just one source of income—they build multiple income streams. That means money comes from different places, reducing the risk of financial struggle.

Here are three types of income streams you should consider:

ACTIVE INCOME –

Money you earn from working a job or running a business. *(Example: Babysitting, selling products, freelancing.)*

PASSIVE INCOME –

Money that keeps coming in even when you're not actively working. *(Example: Selling digital products, earning ad revenue from YouTube, renting out property.)*

PORTFOLIO INCOME –

Money from investments like stocks, bonds, or real estate. *(Example: Buying shares in a company and earning dividends.)*

HOW TO START?

1. Pick One –

Start with an active income, then reinvest profits into passive or portfolio income.

2. Scale Up –

Once one income stream is stable, add another.

3. Stay Focused –

Don't try to do everything at once—build step by step.

A future millionaire doesn't just rely on one paycheck. Start thinking of ways to multiply your income!

Do not save what is left after spending, but spend what is left after saving.

WARREN BUFFETT

CHAPTER 3

THE ART OF SAVING AND INVESTING

3. THE ART OF SAVING AND INVESTING

Earning money is only half the equation. How you manage it determines whether you stay broke or build wealth. Many people work hard, make money, and still struggle financially. Why? Because they don't know how to save and invest. Here's the reality:

- **A spender makes money and blows it on things that bring temporary satisfaction.**
- **A wealth builder makes money, saves a portion, and invests it in ways that multiply over time.**

If you want to become financially free, you need to train yourself to be a **wealth builder.**

WHY MOST PEOPLE STAY BROKE

The average person lives paycheck to paycheck, not because they don't make enough, but because they have a bad relationship with money.

Here are some common mistakes that keep people broke:

1. **Spending everything they earn** – No savings, no investments, just living for the moment.
2. **Thinking saving is enough** – Saving is important, but money sitting in a bank won't grow. Investing makes it work for you.
3. **Trying to impress people** – Buying expensive things to show off instead of making wise financial decisions.
4. **Ignoring financial education** – Avoiding books, resources, and mentors who could teach them better money habits.

If you recognize any of these habits in yourself, don't worry. You have the power to change starting today.

THE POWER OF SAVING: PAY YOURSELF FIRST

Most people spend their money first and try to save whatever is left. That's backward thinking. Wealth builders pay themselves first. This means:

1. As soon as you earn money, set aside a portion for saving and investing.
2. Live on what's left—never the other way around.
3. Treat saving like an expense—it's non-negotiable.

A simple way to do this is by following the **10-20-70 Rule:**

- 10% – Give (tithes, charity, generosity)
- 20% – Save and invest
- 70% – Live on (expenses, fun, necessities)

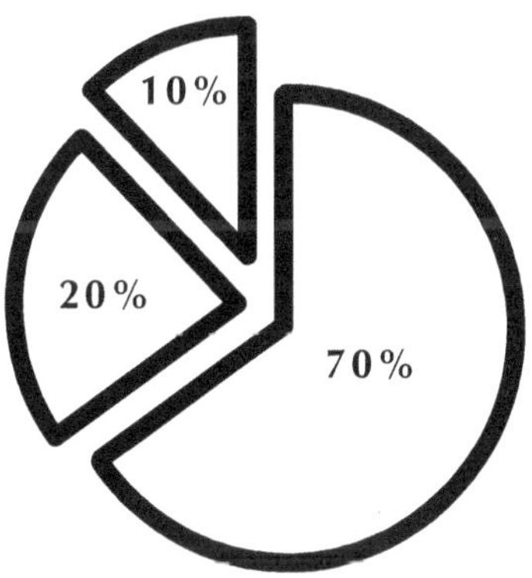

If you start applying this principle now, you'll build financial security faster than most adults!

INVESTING: HOW TO MAKE YOUR MONEY WORK FOR YOU

Saving is important, but saving alone won't make you wealthy. You need to invest so your money can grow.

Think of investing like planting a tree:

- You plant a small seed (your investment).
- Over time, it grows into a strong tree (your wealth).
- Eventually, that tree produces fruit (passive income), and you no longer have to work as hard.

Here are three simple ways to start investing early:

1. START WITH SMALL INVESTMENTS –

You don't need thousands of dollars to invest. Many platforms allow you to start with as little as $5-$50.

2. THINK LONG-TERM –

Real wealth comes from consistent investing over time. Don't rush—let your money grow.

3. KEEP LEARNING –

Read books, follow financial experts, and keep increasing your knowledge. The more you know, the better your decisions will be.

HOW TO START RESEARCHING INVESTMENTS

Investing might sound complicated, but the truth is, anyone can learn how to invest wisely—even as a teen! You don't need thousands of dollars to start. The key is to learn about investing early, so when the time comes, you'll be ready to make smart financial moves.

Here's how you can start researching investments today:

1. LEARN THE BASICS

Before putting money into anything, understand how investing works. Here are some beginner-friendly ways to learn:

- **Books** – Read books on investing, such as Rich Dad Poor Dad and The Psychology of Money.

- **Videos & Podcasts** – Watch YouTube videos or listen to podcasts that explain investing in simple terms.

- **Online Courses** – Free courses on platforms like Coursera, Khan Academy, and Udemy teach investing fundamentals.

2. EXPLORE DIFFERENT TYPES OF INVESTMENTS

Not all investments are the same. Some grow slowly but are safe, while others are risky but can make more money.

Here are a few investment types to research:

- **Stocks** – Buying shares of a company and earning money if the company grows.

- **Real Estate** – Investing in property to rent or sell for a profit.

- **Starting a Business** – The best way to invest in yourself! Entrepreneurship can generate long-term income.

3. UNDERSTAND THE RISKS & REWARDS

Every investment has some level of risk. Before investing in anything, ask yourself:

- How does this investment make money?
- What happens if the value goes down?
- Is this a short-term or long-term investment?

Pro Tip: Investing is **NOT** about "getting rich quick." It's about making smart decisions that grow your money over time.

4. START SMALL (WHEN YOU'RE READY!)

Many investment platforms allow you to start with just $5 or $10. You don't need to rush, but as you learn, you can practice by saving up for your first investment—even if it's just a small amount!

5. FIND A MENTOR OR TRUSTED SOURCE

The best investors learn from people who are already successful. If you know an adult who invests wisely, ask them questions. Learn from their experiences!

Even if you're not ready to invest yet, learning about investing NOW will put you ahead of most adults. By the time you're earning your own money, you'll know exactly how to make your money work for you instead of just spending it!

BE THE MASTER, NOT THE SLAVE

Proverbs 22:7 (KJV) says, ***"The rich ruleth over the poor, and the borrower is servant to the lender."***

If you don't control your money, your money will control you.

- Saving teaches discipline.
- Investing teaches growth.
- Both create freedom.

The question is: Will you master your finances, or will money rule your life? The choice is yours.

Train yourself now to save and invest wisely, and you'll never have to live paycheck to paycheck. You'll be building a future most people only dream of.

QUIZ!

CHAPTER 3 QUIZ: THE ART OF SAVING AND INVESTING

1. What is the main reason many people struggle financially even though they make money?

A) They don't work enough hours
B) They forget to pay taxes
C) They don't know how to save and invest
D) They hide their money

2. Who is a wealth builder?

A) Someone who spends all their money quickly
B) Someone who makes money and uses it for fun
C) Someone who saves and invests their money
D) Someone who waits for a big break

3. Which of the following is NOT a reason people stay broke?

A) Spending everything they earn
B) Investing too early
C) Trying to impress others
D) Ignoring financial education

4. What does "pay yourself first" mean?

A) Spend all your money before giving or saving
B) Save and invest before spending on anything else
C) Always buy yourself something nice
D) Pay your bills last

5. According to the 10-20-70 Rule, what does the "20" stand for?

A) 20% for clothes
B) 20% for food and fun
C) 20% for savings and investing
D) 20% for phone bills

6. What is one of the best ways to make your money grow over time?

A) Hiding it under your bed
B) Keeping it in a checking account
C) Investing it
D) Spending it as soon as you earn it

7. Which of these is considered a type of investment?

A) Shopping
B) Stocks

C) Video games
D) Allowance

8. Why is it important to learn about investing before actually doing it?

A) To make friends
B) So you can avoid doing chores
C) To make smart decisions and avoid risks
D) To get rich quickly

9. What is one place teens can start learning about investing?

A) TikTok trends
B) YouTube, podcasts, or books
C) Shopping malls
D) Music videos

10. What does Proverbs 22:7 say about money and borrowing?

A) Saving is boring
B) You must spend to live
C) The borrower is servant to the lender
D) Wealth doesn't matter

A budget is telling your money where to go instead of wondering where it went.

JOHN C. MAXWELL

CHAPTER 4

SMART SPENDING HABITS

4. SMART SPENDING HABITS

IT'S NOT ABOUT HOW MUCH YOU MAKE—IT'S ABOUT HOW MUCH YOU KEEP

Most people believe that the secret to wealth is making more money. But here's the truth: Even if you earn a million dollars, you can still be broke if you don't know how to manage it.

Think about it—there are celebrities and athletes who made millions yet lost everything. Why? Because they spent recklessly. They thought making more money would solve their problems, but they never learned how to spend wisely. Financial success isn't just about how much money comes in—it's about how you manage what goes out.

WHY MOST PEOPLE STRUGGLE WITH MONEY

Have you ever heard someone say, "I just don't know where my money goes!"? That's a sign of poor spending habits.

Here's what keeps people trapped in financial struggle:

1. **Impulse buying** – Spending money on things they don't need just because they "feel like it."
2. **Trying to impress others** – Buying name-brand clothes, expensive gadgets, or luxury items just to look rich.
3. **Not having a budget** – Spending blindly without a plan, then wondering why they're broke.
4. **Borrowing to maintain a lifestyle** – Using credit cards or loans to buy things they can't afford.

The good news? You don't have to fall into these traps. If you develop smart spending habits early, you'll avoid financial stress and build a solid future.

As a teenager, the impulse to buy things can be strong, but making thoughtful choices now will set you up for success down the road.

NEEDS VS. WANTS: THE KEY TO FINANCIAL CONTROL

One of the biggest mistakes people make is not knowing the difference between a need and a want.

A need is something essential—food, shelter, clothing, education, transportation.

A want is something extra—designer shoes, the latest phone, eating out every week, luxury vacations. Here's how to stay in control of your spending:

Before buying something, ask yourself:

- Do I really need this, or do I just want it?
- Will this add value to my life, or is it just temporary excitement?
- If I don't buy this, will my life be any worse?

Most of the time, what we think we "need" is really just a want. When you learn to say NO to unnecessary spending, you say YES to financial freedom.

HOW TO BUDGET WITHOUT FEELING RESTRICTED

Some people hear the word budget and think, "That means I can't enjoy life." But that's not true. A budget doesn't limit you—it frees you.

A budget gives you:

- **Control** – You know exactly where your money is going.
- **Peace of mind** – No more wondering if you have enough.
- **More money** – Because you're not wasting it on things that don't matter.

Here's a simple way to budget:

1. KNOW YOUR INCOME –

List how much money you make from all sources.

2. TRACK YOUR EXPENSES –

Write down everything you spend for a month.

3. CUT UNNECESSARY SPENDING –

Find areas where you can spend less.

4. SET SPENDING LIMITS –

Decide how much you'll spend on different categories (food, entertainment, shopping, etc.).

5. STICK TO THE PLAN –

Self-discipline is the key to success.

AVOIDING LIFESTYLE CREEP: DON'T LET MORE MONEY LEAD TO MORE PROBLEMS

Many people think that once they start making more money, their problems will disappear. But the truth is, the more you earn, the easier it is to spend mindlessly. This is called lifestyle creep—when your spending increases as your income grows.

Example: You start making an extra $200 per month. Instead of saving or investing it, you upgrade your phone, eat out more, and suddenly... you're still broke!

HOW TO AVOID LIFESTYLE CREEP:

1. **Live below your means** – Just because you can afford it doesn't mean you need it.
2. **Increase your savings as your income grows** – If you get a raise or earn extra money, save or invest first before spending.
3. **Think before upgrading** – Do you really need the newest phone, or is your current one working fine?

Building wealth is not about how much you make —it's about how much you keep!

DON'T LET MONEY CONTROL YOU—TAKE CONTROL OF YOUR MONEY

Money is a tool—it should work for you, not the other way around. If you learn to control your spending now, you'll never have to worry about being broke.

Proverbs 21:20 (KJV) says, ***"There is treasure to be desired and oil in the dwelling of the wise; but a foolish man spendeth it up."*** Wise people know how to manage their money. Foolish people spend everything they have

QUIZ!

CHAPTER 4 QUIZ: SMART SPENDING HABITS

1. Why can someone who earns a million dollars still end up broke?

A) They don't have a college degree
B) They never get a promotion
C) They don't know how to manage their money
D) They give too much to charity

2. What is one of the most common poor money habits mentioned in this chapter?

A) Buying food at the supermarket
B) Tracking expenses
C) Impulse buying
D) Investing too early

3. Which of the following is a need and not a want?

A) Designer shoes
B) The latest phone
C) Transportation to school
D) Luxury vacation

4. What is the key benefit of creating a budget?

A) It stops you from spending money altogether
B) It limits your fun
C) It gives you freedom and control over your money
D) It makes you rich overnight

5. What is "lifestyle creep"?

A) A budgeting method
B) When your spending increases as your income increases
C) When your money disappears due to inflation
D) A person who spends all your money

6. What's a smart first step to avoid lifestyle creep?

A) Buy more expensive items
B) Spend before saving
C) Live below your means
D) Get a new credit card

7. According to the chapter, wealthy people follow a budget because:

A) They want to show off
B) They're boring

C) They know every dollar has a job
D) They don't trust banks

8. What does it mean to "track your expenses"?

A) Check how much your friends spend
B) Write down what you spend your money on
C) Only spend money on weekends
D) Guess your monthly spending

9. What does Proverbs 21:20 say about spending?

A) "A wise man saves; a foolish man spends it all."
B) "Money grows on trees."
C) "He who waits will be wealthy."
D) "The borrower is servant to the lender."

10. What should you ask before buying something?

A) Will this go viral on TikTok?
B) Do I have enough space in my closet?
C) Do I need this or just want it?
D) Will my friends like it?

“

Financial freedom is available to those who learn about it and work for it.

ROBERT KIYOSAKI

”

CHAPTER 5

THE FUTURE MILLIONAIRE'S BLUEPRINT

5. THE FUTURE MILLIONAIRE'S BLUEPRINT

WEALTH DOESN'T HAPPEN BY ACCIDENT—IT'S BUILT WITH A PLAN

Every skyscraper begins with a blueprint. No architect wakes up one day and randomly starts stacking bricks, hoping a masterpiece will appear. They plan every detail before the first brick is laid.

Wealth works the same way. You don't become a millionaire by accident—you build it with a strategy.

Most people wander through life financially unprepared, hoping money will "work itself out." But hope is not a financial strategy.

If you want to create real wealth, you need a blueprint—a step-by-step plan that will guide you from where you are now to where you want to be.

STEP 1: DEFINE YOUR FINANCIAL GOALS

You can't build wealth if you don't know what you're working toward. What does financial success look like to you?

1. Do you want to be debt-free and never worry about bills?
2. Do you want to own a business and create multiple streams of income?
3. Do you want to retire early and have money working for you?
4. Do you want to build generational wealth for your family?

Write down your short-term, mid-term, and long-term financial goals. ***(Note: Adjust the currency to match your country's standard for accurate financial planning)***

- **Short-term:** Save $1,000 USD, start a business, invest $500 USD.

- **Mid-term:** Buy a car with cash, have $10,000 USD saved.

- **Long-term:** Own real estate, have passive income, retire early.

A goal without a plan is just a wish. So, once you set your goals, create a clear path to achieve them.

STEP 2: CREATE MULTIPLE STREAMS OF INCOME

Millionaires don't rely on just one source of income—they create multiple streams.

If you depend on just one paycheck, you're one emergency away from financial stress. That's why it's important to develop different ways to make money.

Here are a few income streams you can start building today:

1. A Side Hustle – Selling products, tutoring, freelancing, or offering services.

2. Investments – Stocks, real estate, or starting a small business.

3. Passive Income – Writing a book, creating an online course, or monetizing a skill.

Even if you start small, small streams grow into rivers of wealth.

STEP 3: BUILD A STRONG MONEY MANAGEMENT SYSTEM

Making money is one thing—keeping and growing it is another. You need a money management system that keeps you in control.

Here's a simple system to follow:

1. **Give first** – Tithe, give to charity, or support a cause. Generosity opens doors.
2. **Save and invest** – Before spending, put money toward savings and investments.
3. **Spend wisely** – Budget for needs first, then allocate for wants.
4. **Avoid debt** – Stay away from **unnecessary** loans and credit card debt.

If you manage $100 USD well, you'll manage $1,000 USD well. If you waste $100 USD, you'll waste $1,000 USD. Start practicing good habits now.

STEP 4: SURROUND YOURSELF WITH FINANCIALLY WISE PEOPLE

The people around you influence your financial mindset. If you hang around broke-minded people, you'll think like them. If you surround yourself with wealth-minded people, you'll learn, grow, and level up.

Look for mentors, books, and communities that challenge you to think bigger. **Proverbs 13:20 (KJV)** says, ***"He that walketh with wise men shall be wise: but a companion of fools shall be destroyed."*** Your future is shaped by who you learn from. Choose wisely.

STEP 5: STAY DISCIPLINED AND CONSISTENT

Building wealth takes time. It's not an overnight success—it's a lifetime journey.

Most people fail because they get impatient. They want quick money, and when things don't happen fast enough, they quit. But real success belongs to those who are consistent.

Stick to your plan. Keep learning. Keep growing. Keep building. Your future millionaire self will thank you.

THE FOUNDATION OF YOUR FINANCIAL FUTURE STARTS TODAY

Everything you need to become successful is already in your hands—you just need to take action.

- Dream big.
- Make a plan.
- Be disciplined.
- Stay focused.

Your millionaire future isn't far away—it starts with the choices you make right now.

Are you ready to build the life you deserve? Then start today.

QUIZ!

CHAPTER 5 QUIZ: THE FUTURE MILLIONAIRE'S BLUEPRINT

1. What is the purpose of a financial blueprint?

A) To decorate your vision board
B) To create a random spending plan
C) To guide you from where you are to where you want to be
D) To help you avoid budgeting

2. What does the chapter compare building wealth to?

A) Building a sandcastle
B) Building a friendship
C) Building a skyscraper
D) Building a shopping list

3. Which of these is an example of a long-term financial goal?

A) Save $1,000 USD
B) Buy a car
C) Start a business
D) Own real estate and retire early

4. Why is having multiple streams of income important?

A) It makes you look busy
B) It guarantees instant success
C) It protects you from financial emergencies
D) It makes budgeting unnecessary

5. What is an example of passive income?

A) Selling snacks at school
B) Freelancing for a client
C) Writing a book that continues to earn money
D) Babysitting every weekend

6. What should you do before spending money, according to the chapter's money management system?

A) Buy your favorite item
B) Save and invest
C) Ask a friend
D) Take out a loan

7. What does Proverbs 13:20 say about the people you spend time with?

A) "Birds of a feather save together."
B) "Walk with the wise and become wise."

C) "Spend wisely or fall deeply."
D) "Money comes to those who wait."

8. What happens if you mismanage $100, according to the book?

A) You'll have fun
B) You'll learn from it instantly
C) You're likely to mismanage $1,000 too
D) You'll lose friends

9. Why do most people fail at building wealth?

A) They don't want money
B) They're too young
C) They get impatient and quit too soon
D) They invest too much

10. What is the final encouragement given at the end of the chapter?

A) "Take risks without thinking."
B) "Start tomorrow after a long break."
C) "Your future millionaire self
will thank you—start today."
D) "Money solves everything."

Success is not in what you have, but who you are.

BO BENNETT

CHAPTER 6

GIVING AND GENEROSITY

6. GIVING AND GENEROSITY

THE WEALTHY UNDERSTAND THIS SECRET

If you study the habits of truly wealthy people, you'll notice something surprising: They are givers.

Many people believe that giving money away will make them poorer, but the opposite is true. Giving is a principle of increase. It's a law that works just like planting seeds—when you sow, you reap.

Luke 6:38 (KJV) says, ***"Give, and it shall be given unto you; good measure, pressed down, and shaken together, and running over, shall men give into your bosom..."***

This is not just a spiritual truth—it's a financial one. The more generous you are, the more blessings and opportunities flow back into your life.

WHY SOME PEOPLE STRUGGLE WITH GIVING

Many people hesitate to give because they believe:

- ***"I don't have enough to give."***
- ***"I need to take care of myself first."***
- ***"If I give, I'll have less."***

But here's the truth: Giving isn't about the amount—it's about the mindset.

Even if you only have $10 USD, setting aside a small portion to bless someone else changes your perspective on money. It teaches you that money is a tool, not a master. It reminds you that true wealth isn't about what you keep, but what you're able to share.

THE POWER OF TITHING AND GENEROSITY

Tithing, giving the first 10% of your income to God, has been a foundational financial principle for centuries. It's an act of faith and obedience that demonstrates your trust in God as your Provider.

Malachi 3:10 (KJV) says, ***"Bring ye all the tithes into the storehouse, that there may be meat in mine house, and prove me now herewith, saith the LORD of hosts, if I will not open you the windows of heaven, and pour you out a blessing, that there shall not be room enough to receive it."***

God promises that when you give, He will bless you abundantly. But beyond tithing, generosity should be a lifestyle. Giving doesn't just mean donating to a church—it means helping those in need, supporting causes, and making a difference wherever you can.

THE WEALTHY GIVE FOR A REASON

Successful business owners, investors, and entrepreneurs understand that the more they give, the more they receive.

Why? Because:

- **Giving keeps your heart in the right place**—it stops greed from taking over.
- **Giving builds trust with people**—they see you as someone who cares.
- **Giving opens doors**—many wealthy people get opportunities simply because they were generous.

If you want to build wealth, don't wait until you're rich to start giving. Start now, even if it's small.

WAYS TO GIVE—EVEN WITHOUT MONEY

Maybe you don't have much money to give right now. That's okay! You can still practice generosity.

Here's how:

- **Give your time** – Volunteer, help someone in need, serve at your church.

- **Give your skills** – Offer your talents to help others grow.

- **Give encouragement** – Speak life into others, support their dreams.

- **Give kindness** – Be someone who uplifts, not just takes.

Generosity isn't about how much money you have—it's about your willingness to bless others with what you do have.

THE HEART OF A MILLIONAIRE IS A HEART OF GIVING

Many people chase money, but true millionaires understand that wealth is about impact. When you bless others, you create a life that is fulfilling, joyful, and full of divine favor.

Proverbs 11:25 (KJV) says, ***"The liberal soul shall be made fat: and he that watereth shall be watered also himself."*** In other words, when you give, you never run dry. Your generosity sets you up for abundance in ways you can't even imagine.

So, as you build your financial future, don't just ask, "How much money can I make?" Ask, "How much impact can I create?"

The true measure of wealth is not what you keep—it's what you give away.

QUIZ!

CHAPTER 6 QUIZ: GIVING AND GENEROSITY

1. What do truly wealthy people tend to be?

A) Risk-takers
B) Givers
C) Hoarders
D) Minimalists

2. According to Luke 6:38, what happens when you give?

A) It will be given back to you abundantly
B) Others will owe you
C) You become poor
D) You'll be seen as weak

3. What is a common myth about giving?

A) Giving will make you popular
B) Giving builds discipline
C) You need to be rich to give
D) Giving helps you learn budgeting

4. Why is tithing considered important in this chapter?

A) It supports the local economy
B) It shows generosity to friends
C) It's optional depending on how you feel
D) It is an act of faith and obedience

5. What does Malachi 3:10 promise to those who tithe?

A) They will be respected
B) They will never get sick
C) God will pour out blessings they can't contain
D) They will get better jobs

6. Why do wealthy people often give?

A) To avoid taxes
B) To impress others
C) To open doors and maintain the right mindset
D) To appear generous without meaning it

7. Which of the following is NOT a way to give mentioned in the chapter?

A) Give your kindness
B) Give your time

C) Give your budget
D) Give your skills

8. What does generosity help guard your heart against?

A) Greed
B) Doubt
C) Laziness
D) Jealousy

9. What does the chapter say is the true measure of wealth?

A) How much you save
B) How many investments you have
C) The size of your house
D) What you give away

10. What should you ask yourself while building your financial future?

A) "How quickly can I get rich?"
B) "How much money can I keep?"
C) "How much impact can I create?"
D) "How much more can I earn than my friends?"

If you don't find a way to make money while you sleep, you will work until you die.

WARREN BUFFETT

CHAPTER 7

AVOIDING FINANCIAL PITFALLS

7. AVOIDING FINANCIAL PITFALLS

IT'S NOT JUST ABOUT MAKING MONEY —IT'S ABOUT KEEPING IT

Many people make good money but still struggle financially. Why? Because what you don't know can hurt you.

Wealth isn't just about how much you earn—it's about how well you manage what you have. Some of the biggest financial mistakes can keep you stuck in a cycle of frustration, no matter how much money you make.

The good news? You don't have to learn the hard way. By recognizing these common financial pitfalls now, you can avoid the mistakes that keep most people broke.

PITFALL #1: LIVING BEYOND YOUR MEANS

One of the fastest ways to financial failure is spending more than you earn. It doesn't matter if you make $1,000 USD a month or $10,000 USD a month—if your expenses are higher than your income, you will always be broke.

Signs you're living beyond your means:

- You run out of money before payday.
- You rely on credit cards or loans to survive.
- You buy expensive things just to "keep up" with others.

PITFALL #2: NOT HAVING AN EMERGENCY FUND

Life happens—unexpected bills, car repairs, medical expenses. If you're not prepared, one financial emergency can throw you into debt.

Experts recommend saving at least three to six months' worth of expenses in an emergency fund. But if that seems overwhelming, start small.

Even saving $500 USD to $1,000 USD as a safety net can prevent you from falling into financial hardship.

PITFALL #3: USING DEBT AS A CRUTCH

Debt can be a financial trap that keeps you working for money instead of making money work for you. **Not all debt is bad**—for example, taking out a loan to invest in a business can be strategic. But using debt to fund your lifestyle, buy things you don't need, or impress people? That's a recipe for financial disaster.

SIGNS OF DANGEROUS DEBT:

1. Paying only the minimum on credit card balances.
2. Borrowing money for things that don't increase in value.
3. Taking loans just to "keep up" with a certain lifestyle.

PITFALL #4: FAILING TO INVEST

Many people work hard for money but never let their money work for them. They save, but they don't invest, and they miss out on opportunities to build wealth.

The problem?

Money sitting in a savings account isn't growing. In fact, with inflation, your money is losing value over time.

PITFALL #5: LACK OF FINANCIAL EDUCATION

One of the biggest financial mistakes is not taking the time to learn about money. The difference between those who struggle and those who thrive financially isn't luck—**it's knowledge.** Wealthy people study money, learn from experts, and apply what they learn.

Proverbs 4:7 (KJV) says, ***"Wisdom is the principal thing; therefore get wisdom: and with all thy getting get understanding."***

The more you understand money, the better your financial future will be.

SUCCESS IS ABOUT WHAT YOU DO—AND WHAT YOU AVOID

Avoiding financial pitfalls is just as important as making smart money moves.

- Live below your means.
- Save for emergencies.
- Stay out of unnecessary debt.
- Invest your money wisely.
- Keep learning about finances.

If you can avoid these common traps, you'll be ahead of 90% of people financially. The road to wealth isn't just about making money—it's about keeping it, growing it, and using it wisely.

Your financial future is in your hands. Make wise choices now, and you'll enjoy the rewards later.

QUIZ!

CHAPTER 7 QUIZ: AVOIDING FINANCIAL PITFALLS

1. What is one of the biggest financial mistakes people make?

A) Saving too much
B) Not investing in luxury items
C) Living beyond their means
D) Working too many jobs

2. What's a clear sign that you're living beyond your means?

A) You always have money left at the end of the month
B) You track all your spending
C) You run out of money before payday
D) You avoid buying name-brand items

3. Why is having an emergency fund important?

A) So you can shop when you're bored
B) To handle unexpected expenses without going into debt
C) To invest in risky stocks
D) To lend money to friends

4. How much should you aim to save in an emergency fund according to the chapter?

A) $50
B) At least three to six months' worth of expenses
C) One month of rent
D) Half your income

5. What kind of debt is considered dangerous?

A) A loan to start a business
B) Credit card debt for luxury purchases
C) A mortgage on a home
D) A student loan

6. What is a sign of dangerous debt?

A) Paying your bills early
B) Using a credit card only for gas
C) Paying only the minimum on your credit card
D) Borrowing to invest in your education

7. What happens if you only save and don't invest?

A) Your money will still grow faster than inflation
B) Your money will lose value over time

C) You'll become rich faster
D) You don't need to worry about inflation

8. What is the main reason many people never build wealth, even if they earn well?

A) They don't travel
B) They don't know how to manage money
C) They spend too much time studying
D) They avoid all types of debt

9. According to the chapter, what sets wealthy people apart?

A) Their family background
B) Their luck
C) Their financial education
D) Their fashion sense

10. What does Proverbs 4:7 teach us about financial wisdom?

A) Focus on saving first
B) Seek out job promotions
C) Wisdom is the principal thing—get understanding
D) Invest only in real estate

Wealth is the ability to fully experience life.

HENRY DAVID THOREAU

CHAPTER 8

FINANCIAL FREEDOM AND LEGACY

8. FINANCIAL FREEDOM AND LEGACY

WHAT DOES TRUE FINANCIAL FREEDOM LOOK LIKE?

Financial freedom is not just about having a lot of money—it's about having control over your time, your choices, and your future.

It means:

- You don't have to live paycheck to paycheck.
- You can take care of your family without stress.
- You can give generously without worrying about your own needs.

You have money working for you instead of working for money.

Many people believe financial freedom is only for the wealthy, but the truth is, anyone can achieve it by making smart financial decisions early in life.

STEP 1: DEFINE WHAT FINANCIAL FREEDOM MEANS FOR YOU

For some, financial freedom means having enough passive income so they never have to work again. For others, it means being debt-free and stress-free.

What does financial freedom look like to you?

Take a moment and write it down. The clearer your vision, the more likely you are to achieve it.

STEP 2: CREATE A PATH TO FINANCIAL INDEPENDENCE

If you want financial freedom, you need a plan to get there. Here are five key steps:

1. **Live Below Your Means** – Spend less than you earn and invest the difference.
2. **Eliminate Debt** – Pay off high-interest debt so your money isn't going to lenders.
3. **Build Multiple Streams of Income** – Don't rely on just one paycheck—find ways to make money in different areas.
4. **Invest Consistently** – The sooner you start investing, the sooner your money starts working for you.
5. **Have a Long-Term Wealth Strategy** – Plan for retirement, real estate, and business opportunities that will give you lasting income.

If you stick to this path, financial freedom won't be just a dream—it will be your reality.

STEP 3: THINK BEYOND YOURSELF—BUILD A LEGACY

Financial freedom isn't just about enjoying life for yourself. It's about leaving something behind for future generations.

Proverbs 13:22 (KJV) says, *"A good man leaveth an inheritance to his children's children..."*

This means:

- Teaching your children and family how to handle money wisely.

- Building assets like businesses, investments, and real estate that can benefit generations after you.

- Living in a way that impacts and blesses others.

Your financial journey is bigger than you—it's about creating wealth that lasts.

STEP 4: MAKE SURE MONEY DOESN'T BECOME YOUR MASTER

It's possible to achieve financial success but still lose sight of what truly matters. Many people work so hard for money that they:

- Neglect their faith.

- Lose their families.

- Forget the importance of giving.

Financial freedom is powerful, but it should never take the place of God, family, and purpose.

Matthew 6:33 (KJV) reminds us, ***"But seek ye first the kingdom of God, and his righteousness; and all these things shall be added unto you."***

When you put God first, money becomes a tool, not an idol.

YOU WERE BORN TO PROSPER—START NOW

Financial freedom is not reserved for a lucky few—it's for those who are disciplined, wise, and willing to learn.

You have the power to create wealth, break generational curses, and build a future of abundance. But it starts **NOW.**

- Make a plan.
- Stay focused.
- Keep growing.
- Leave a legacy.

Your future millionaire self is depending on you. Will you take the steps today to secure the life you desire tomorrow?

The choice is yours. Start building your financial freedom now!

QUIZ!

CHAPTER 8 QUIZ: FINANCIAL FREEDOM AND LEGACY

1. What does true financial freedom mean?

A) Having millions of dollars in the bank
B) Being able to quit your job immediately
C) Having control over your time, choices, and future
D) Buying everything you want without thinking

2. Which of the following is NOT a sign of financial freedom?

A) Living paycheck to paycheck
B) Taking care of your family without stress
C) Giving generously without fear
D) Having money work for you

3. What is the first step to achieving financial freedom?

A) Getting a high-paying job
B) Defining what financial freedom means for you
C) Avoiding credit cards
D) Winning the lottery

4. What does it mean to "live below your means"?

A) Spend exactly what you earn
B) Spend less than you earn and invest the rest
C) Spend more now and save later
D) Avoid paying bills

5. Why is it important to build multiple streams of income?

A) To show off your success
B) To rely on just one paycheck
C) To avoid taxes
D) To reduce financial risk and increase income sources

6. What does Proverbs 13:22 teach about legacy?

A) Money should only be used for enjoyment
B) A good person leaves an inheritance for future generations
C) You shouldn't worry about saving
D) Generosity is unnecessary

7. What is one way to build a lasting legacy?

A) Spend all your money before retirement
B) Teach your family how to handle money

C) Keep your financial knowledge to yourself
D) Avoid investing

8. What's the danger of letting money become your master?

A) You'll never want to work again
B) You'll focus too much on budgeting
C) You may neglect faith, family, and purpose
D) You'll stop saving money

9. According to Matthew 6:33, what should come first in your life?

A) Wealth accumulation
B) Business success
C) The kingdom of God and His righteousness
D) Buying a home

10. What should you do today to start building financial freedom?

A) Wait until you're older
B) Make a plan, stay focused, and keep growing
C) Copy what others are doing
D) Spend your money and enjoy life now

> It takes 20 years to build a reputation and five minutes to ruin it. If you think about that, you'll do things differently.

WARREN BUFFETT

CHAPTER 9

CREDIT SCORES 101

9. CREDIT SCORES 101

WHAT EVERY FUTURE MILLIONAIRE SHOULD KNOW

A credit score is a number—usually between 300 and 850—that shows how trustworthy you are when it comes to borrowing and repaying money. The higher your score, the better.

WHY DOES IT MATTER?

Your credit score can impact many major life decisions. It affects:

- Whether you can get approved for a loan (car, home, or business)
- How much interest you'll pay
- Your ability to rent an apartment

- Whether you qualify for a credit card or phone plan

Good credit opens doors. Bad credit can lock you out of financial opportunities.

HOW IS A CREDIT SCORE BUILT?

Even if you're not using credit yet, understanding how it works helps you prepare.

Here are the key factors that shape your credit score:

1. **Payment History** – Pay all bills on time. Even a late payment can lower your score.
2. **Credit Usage** – Use only a small portion of your credit limit. Keeping balances low shows responsibility.
3. **Length of Credit History** – The longer you've had credit, the better. Starting early (even as an authorized user) helps.
4. **Types of Credit** – Having a mix of credit cards, loans, or student debt shows you can manage different accounts.
5. **New Credit Applications** – Applying for too many accounts in a short time can signal financial stress and hurt your score.

SMART MOVES FOR TEENS

You may not be using credit yet, but these smart habits will help you build a solid foundation:

- **Save consistently** – Develop financial discipline early.
- **Create a budget** – Practice managing your money before handling credit.
- **Talk to a parent or guardian** – When the time is right, becoming an authorized user on their credit card can help you start building credit.
- **Avoid borrowing for wants** – Only borrow for things that add long-term value.

A credit score is like a financial reputation—it takes time to build, but only moments to damage. Start now by managing your money wisely. When it's time to use credit, you'll be ready.

Financial success starts with intention—every smart move you make today is building the millionaire you're becoming.

QUIZ!

CHAPTER 9 QUIZ:
CREDIT SCORES 101

1. What is the typical range of a credit score?

A) 100–500
B) 200–800
C) 300–850
D) 400–900

2. What does a higher credit score usually indicate?

A) You don't borrow money
B) You have more friends
C) You're a trustworthy borrower
D) You make more money

3. Which of the following is the MOST important factor in your credit score?

A) Credit card limit
B) Payment history
C) Number of jobs
D) Monthly income

4. True or False: Missing even one payment can lower your credit score.

A) True
B) False

5. What is a smart way to use credit if you get a credit card in the future?

A) Use the full limit every month
B) Only make the minimum payment
C) Max it out quickly
D) Use only a small portion of your limit

6. What does "length of credit history" mean?

A) How long you've had a job
B) How long you've been using credit
C) How long it takes to repay debt
D) How long your credit card is

7. Why should you avoid applying for too many credit cards at once?

A) It confuses the bank
B) It makes you look wealthy
C) It can hurt your credit score
D) It increases your credit score

8. What is one way a teen can start building credit early?

A) Borrowing money from friends
B) Getting a car loan
C) Becoming an authorized user on a parent's credit card
D) Paying for everything in cash

9. What's a good reason to borrow money?

A) To impress your friends
B) For things that add long-term value
C) To buy snacks
D) Because you're bored

10. Complete this sentence: A credit score is like a ______.

A) Test grade
B) Password
C) Financial reputation
D) Lottery ticket

Every step you take today is building the wealth you'll walk in tomorrow.

CHELETA BUDDO-GAYLE

YOUR FINANCIAL ROADMAP: A SIMPLE PLAN FOR WEALTH BUILDING

Success in money management comes down to consistency. Here's your simple roadmap:

- **START NOW:** Open a savings account, track your expenses, and learn about money.
- **EARN SMART:** Find ways to make money—side hustles, business, or part-time work.
- **SAVE FIRST, THEN SPEND:** Always pay yourself first before spending on wants.
- **AVOID DEBT:** Only borrow money if necessary and always have a plan to repay.
- **INVEST EARLY**: Even small investments grow over time. Learn about stocks and assets.
- **GIVE BACK:** A millionaire mindset isn't just about making money—it's about blessing others, too

YOUR FINANCIAL ROADMAP

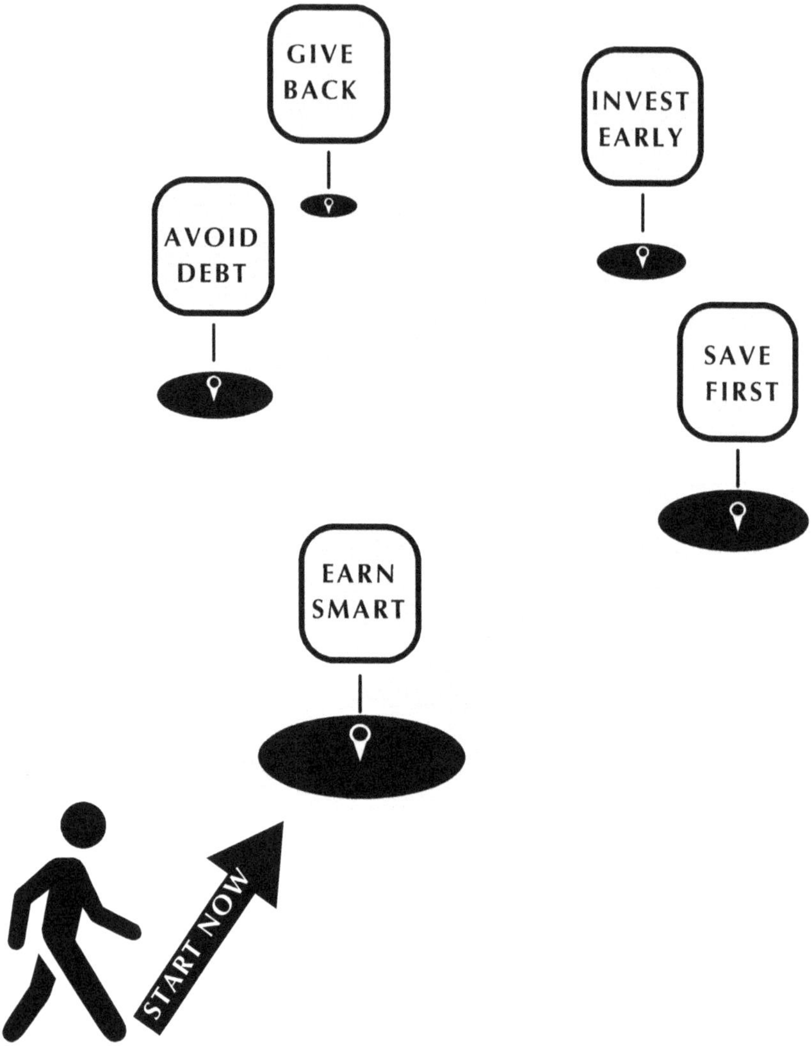

Your future self is depending on you. Will you take the right steps today?

INSPIRING TEEN ENTREPRENEURS

REAL SUCCESS STORIES

INSPIRING TEEN ENTREPRENEURS

REAL SUCCESS STORIES

(Source: Oxford Royale – oxford-royale.com)

These young entrepreneurs prove that age is just a number when it comes to financial success. Here are seven inspiring stories of teenagers who turned ideas into thriving businesses:

1. SHUBHAM BANERJEE – BRAIGO LABS

At just 13 years old, Shubham Banerjee built an affordable Braille printer using a Lego robotics kit, cutting costs from over $2,000 to just $350. His invention led to the creation of Braigo Labs, a company that makes assistive technologies for the visually impaired. His innovation attracted major investors, including Intel, and inspired young inventors worldwide.

2. BELLA TIPPING – KIDZCATIONZ.COM

At 12 years old, Bella Tipping created Kidzcationz, a travel review website for kids, by kids. She wanted to give young travelers a voice, allowing them to rate hotels, restaurants, and attractions. Her platform quickly gained media attention and became a trusted source for family-friendly travel advice.

3. OLLIE FORSYTH – OLLIE'S SHOP & THE BUDDING ENTREPRENEUR CLUB

Diagnosed with dyslexia and bullied in school, 13-year-old Ollie Forsyth turned his struggles into an entrepreneurial journey. He launched Ollie's Shop, an online gift store that made £5,000 within months. He later founded The Budding Entrepreneur Club, connecting young business minds with experienced mentors.

4. NOA MINTZ – NANNIES BY NOA

At just 12 years old, Noa Mintz noticed a gap in quality childcare services in New York. She started Nannies by Noa, a company that matches families with reliable nannies and babysitters. The business grew rapidly, attracting over 190 clients and eventually bringing in professional management to scale operations.

5. MOZIAH BRIDGES – MO'S BOWS

At 9 years old, Moziah Bridges started designing and selling handmade bow ties. His company, Mo's Bows, took off, landing him a deal with Shark Tank's Daymond John and later a contract with the NBA to create bow ties for players. Today, Moziah continues to expand his brand while inspiring other young entrepreneurs.

6. FRASER DOHERTY – SUPERJAM

At 14 years old, Fraser Doherty started making 100% fruit jams using his grandmother's recipes. Within two years, he secured deals with major UK supermarkets, making over $1 million in sales. His business, SuperJam, became a household name, and he later wrote books to encourage young entrepreneurs.

7. RACHEL ZIETZ – GLADIATOR LACROSSE

At 13 years old, Rachel Zietz, a lacrosse player, saw a need for high-quality, affordable lacrosse equipment. She founded Gladiator Lacrosse, a company that quickly grew into a multi-million-dollar business. She was recognized as one of the top young entrepreneurs in the U.S. and continues to inspire female business owners.

These young entrepreneurs prove that age is no barrier to success. With the right mindset, discipline, and financial knowledge, you can start your journey to financial freedom today.

If They Can Do It, So Can You!

Losers quit when they fail. Winners fail until they succeed.

ROBERT KIYOSAKI

OVERCOMING FINANCIAL SETBACKS: MISTAKES ARE NOT THE END

Everyone makes financial mistakes at some point. Maybe you spent all your savings, got into debt, or made a bad business decision. That doesn't mean you failed—it means you're learning!

STEP 1: ACCEPT IT –

Don't waste time feeling guilty. Learn from it and move forward.

STEP 2: ANALYZE WHAT WENT WRONG – ASK YOURSELF:

- Did I overspend on things I didn't need?
- Did I fail to plan my budget properly?
- Did I ignore advice from someone wiser?

STEP 3: CREATE A RECOVERY PLAN –

If you lost money, start saving again. If you got into debt, create a plan to pay it off.

Failure is only failure if you quit. Every setback is a setup for a comeback!

CONCLUSION: YOUR JOURNEY TO WEALTH STARTS NOW

Success Is Built on Daily Decisions

Financial success doesn't happen overnight—it's the result of small, consistent decisions made every single day.

The difference between those who build wealth and those who struggle is not luck—it's discipline, knowledge, and action. You now have the tools, the mindset, and the strategies to start making smart financial choices.

The question is: Will you use them?

WHAT'S YOUR NEXT STEP?

Having knowledge about something is just the beginning. To make real progress, you need to take action.

Here's how you can start right now:

1. SET CLEAR FINANCIAL GOALS –

Write down what you want to achieve with your money and create a plan to get there.

2. TAKE ACTION IMMEDIATELY –

Whether it's starting a side hustle, saving your first $100 USD, or creating a budget, don't wait—start today.

3. KEEP LEARNING AND GROWING –

Financial success is a journey. Keep reading, studying, and surrounding yourself with people who inspire you to grow.

4. STAY DISCIPLINED AND FOCUSED –

There will be distractions, but keep your eyes on the bigger picture. The sacrifices you make today will pay off tomorrow.

5. TRUST GOD AND WALK IN FAITH –

True financial success isn't just about money—it's about purpose, impact, and using wealth to glorify God.

If you commit to this journey, you will see results. There may be setbacks along the way, but don't let them hold you back. Keep pushing forward, and one day, you'll look back and realize that every wise decision you made brought you closer to the financial freedom you've worked so hard for. Stay focused—your future is worth it!

Your financial future is in your hands. Now, go build the life you deserve.

JOURNALING SECTION

REFLECT, PLAN, AND TAKE ACTION

JOURNALING SECTION: REFLECT, PLAN, AND TAKE ACTION

This journaling section will help you reflect on what you've learned, set personal financial goals, and track your progress. It encourages self-awareness, discipline, and intentional action toward financial success.

Note: The pages provided for journaling may be limited. To fully benefit from this book, I encourage you to continue journaling on your own using the principles and templates in this book.

You can use any notebook, digital planner, or even an app to expand on what you've learned. The key is to stay consistent—track your progress, reflect on your financial journey, and take action daily.

Your future millionaire self will thank you!

1. MINDSET REFLECTION:

DEVELOPING THE MILLIONAIRE MINDSET

What are your beliefs about money?

Write down your thoughts on money, wealth, and success. Do you view money as something hard to earn? Do you believe you can be financially successful?

JOURNAL PROMPT:

What is one belief about money that I need to change in order to develop a millionaire mindset?

2. YOUR FIRST MONEY GOALS:

TAKING ACTION

What is your first financial goal?

Think about what you want to achieve financially in the next 3 to 6 months.

JOURNAL PROMPT:

I want to save/invest/earn ____________________

by ____________________ (date). To do this, I will

____

____

3. SMART SPENDING HABITS:

TRACKING PROGRESS

How are you currently spending your money?

Write about your biggest spending habits. Are they helping you reach your financial goals, or are they holding you back?

JOURNAL PROMPT:

One thing I will stop spending money on unnecessarily is ______________________ and instead, I will use that money to __________ ______________________________________

4. GIVING AND GENEROSITY:

CREATING IMPACT

How will you give?

Money is a tool that allows us to bless others.

What is one way you can practice generosity?

JOURNAL PROMPT:

This month, I will give ______________________ to ______________________________________ because I believe in the principle of sowing and reaping.

5. FUTURE VISION:

BUILDING LONG-TERM WEALTH

Where do you see yourself financially in 5 years?

Imagine your future self—a financially free, confident, and successful young person. What does your life look like? How did you get there?

JOURNAL PROMPT:

By the age of ____________, I will have ____________ in savings/investments, I will own ____________, and I will be financially free by ____________.

6. MONTHLY CHECK-IN:

STAYING ON TRACK

At the end of each month, reflect on your progress.

What worked well this month?

What challenges did I face?

One action I will take next month to grow financially is:

BUSINESS PLAN TEMPLATE & BRAINSTORMING GUIDE

BUSINESS PLAN TEMPLATE & BRAINSTORMING GUIDE

This section will help you explore your business ideas, identify your skills and talents, and create a structured plan to turn your vision into reality.

STEP 1: BRAINSTORM YOUR BUSINESS IDEA

Before writing a business plan, answer these questions to discover your skills and potential business ideas:

WHAT ARE YOUR STRENGTHS?

✓ What am I naturally good at? (e.g., drawing, writing, speaking, fixing things)

✓ What do people always compliment me on?

✓ What skills do I already have that could be turned into a business?

WHAT DO YOU ENJOY DOING?

✓ What hobbies or activities make me happy?

✓ If I could do one thing every day and get paid for it, what would it be?

✓ Am I more creative, technical, or hands-on?

WHAT PROBLEMS CAN I SOLVE?

✓ What problems do people around me have that I could solve?

✓ Have I ever created something or provided a service that others needed?

✓ Can I improve an existing product or service?

WHAT BUSINESSES INTEREST ME?

✓ Do I prefer selling products, offering a service, or both?

✓ Would I rather work online, in-person, or both?

✓ Are there businesses I admire that I could learn from?

Use your answers to think of 3-5 potential business ideas!

STEP 2: CHOOSE YOUR BUSINESS IDEA

NOW, PICK ONE BUSINESS IDEA THAT EXCITES YOU THE MOST. USE THESE GUIDING QUESTIONS TO HELP YOU DECIDE:

✓ Does this business align with my skills and interests?

✓ Can I start this business with little or no money?

✓ Is there a demand for this product or service?

Once you've made your choice, move on to **Step 3: Creating Your Business Plan.**

STEP 3: BUSINESS PLAN TEMPLATE

Use this simple business plan template to outline your business idea:

1. BUSINESS NAME & IDEA

- Business Name
- What does my business do?

- Who are my customers? (kids, adults, businesses, schools, etc.)

2. MY PRODUCT OR SERVICE

- What am I selling? (Physical product, digital product, service
- How does it help people?
- What makes my product/service unique?

3. HOW I WILL MAKE MONEY

- How much will I charge?
- Where will I sell? (Online, in person, social media, website, marketplace)
- How will people find me? (Advertising, word of mouth, social media, posters)

4. MY STARTUP COSTS

- Do I need money to start? Yes / No
- What supplies or tools do I need?
- Where can I get them for free or cheap?

5. MY SHORT-TERM & LONG-TERM GOALS

- What do I want to achieve in the first 3 months?

- What do I want to achieve in the first year?

- What is my long-term goal for this business?

YOUNG ENTREPRENEUR

30-DAY FINANCIAL CHALLENGE

YOUNG ENTREPRENEUR: 30-DAY FINANCIAL CHALLENGE & BUSINESS DEVELOPMENT PLAN

This 30-day challenge will help you develop smart financial habits while also guiding you through the process of creating a business plan. By the end of the challenge, you'll have a clear business idea, a structured plan, and a solid financial foundation to start earning and managing money wisely.

Each day includes a small step with an easy-to-understand explanation to help you think like an entrepreneur, manage money wisely, and start taking action.

WEEK 1:
DISCOVERING YOUR BUSINESS IDEA

This week is all about figuring out what kind of business is right for you. You'll explore your skills, hobbies and interests to develop a business idea that fits your strengths. By the end of the week, you will have a clear business concept and an idea of who your customers will be!

DAY 1
IDENTIFY YOUR STRENGTHS AND SKILLS

ACTION!

TAKE A FEW MINUTES TO WRITE DOWN YOUR SKILLS AND TALENTS.

Example: Are you great at art, writing, organizing, fixing things, or talking to people? A business should be built on your strengths, so let's start by identifying them!

DAY 2
WRITE DOWN YOUR HOBBIES & INTERESTS

ACTION!

WRITE DOWN WHAT YOU LOVE TO DO.

Example: Do you love baking? Maybe you could sell cupcakes. Enjoy designing? Maybe you could create social media graphics for small businesses. Write down all your hobbies today—you might find your future business idea in one of them!

DAY 3

LIST 5 BUSINESS IDEAS BASED ON YOUR SKILLS

ACTION!

USING YOUR SKILLS AND HOBBIES, LIST FIVE POSSIBLE BUSINESSES YOU COULD START. DON'T WORRY IF THEY'RE NOT PERFECT—JUST GET IDEAS ON PAPER!

Example: If you love photography, you could sell digital prints or do photo editing for others.

DAY 4

CHOOSE 1 BUSINESS IDEA & DESCRIBE IT IN 1-2 SENTENCES

LOOK AT YOUR LIST AND CHOOSE THE BUSINESS THAT FEELS THE MOST EXCITING AND REALISTIC. NOW, DESCRIBE WHAT YOUR BUSINESS WILL DO IN ONE OR TWO SENTENCES.

Example: "I will create custom greeting cards for birthdays and holidays and sell them online."

DAY 5
IDENTIFY YOUR TARGET CUSTOMERS

ACTION!

WRITE DOWN YOUR IDEAL CUSTOMER AND WHY THEY NEED YOUR BUSINESS.

Example: Are your customers kids, teenagers, parents, or businesses?

DAY 6
RESEARCH SIMILAR BUSINESSES & WRITE DOWN WHAT THEY DO WELL

ACTION!

LOOK AT THREE BUSINESSES THAT ARE SIMILAR TO YOUR IDEA. WRITE DOWN WHAT YOU CAN DO BETTER OR DIFFERENTLY.

Example: What are they doing right? How do they sell their product?

DAY 7

SET A 1-MONTH FINANCIAL GOAL

ACTION!

THINK ABOUT WHAT YOU WANT TO ACHIEVE FINANCIALLY IN YOUR FIRST MONTH. WRITE IT DOWN.

Example: Do you want to make $100 USD? Save $50 USD? Sell 10 products? A clear goal helps you stay focused and motivated!

WEEK 2: PLANNING & BUDGETING

Now that you've chosen a business idea, it's time to plan how to make it a reality. This week focuses on creating a strong foundation by choosing a name, setting a budget and figuring out how to price and market your product and service.

DAY 8

CREATE A BUSINESS NAME & TAGLINE

ACTION!

THINK OF THREE POSSIBLE NAMES FOR YOUR BUSINESS AND CHOOSE YOUR FAVOURITE. THEN, CREATE A TAGLINE (A SHORT SENTENCE THAT DESCRIBES WHAT YOU DO).

Example: "Sweet Bites Bakery – Homemade Treats, Baked with Love."

DAY 9

LIST WHAT YOU NEED TO START

ACTION!

WRITE A LIST OF SUPPLIES, EQUIPMENT, OR SOFTWARE YOU'LL NEED TO START.

Example: Do you need a camera, art supplies, or a website?

DAY 10

RESEARCH COSTS & SET A STARTUP BUDGET

ACTION!

LOOK UP THE PRICES OF THE THINGS ON YOUR LIST. CAN YOU START FOR FREE OR WITH LOW COSTS? IF YOU NEED MONEY, THINK OF WAYS TO GET IT.

Example: Saving, borrowing, or reinvesting profits.

DAY 11

DECIDE HOW MUCH TO CHARGE

ACTION!

RESEARCH HOW MUCH SIMILAR PRODUCTS OR SERVICES COST.

Example: If you buy a bracelet for $3 USD and sell it for $8 USD, you make a profit of $5 USD. Even though you are competing with other businesses, you must ensure you are making a profit so your business can cover expenses and earn you an income.

DAY 12
DECIDE WHERE TO SELL YOUR PRODUCT OR SERVICE

ACTION!

WRITE DOWN THE BEST PLACE TO REACH YOUR CUSTOMERS.

Example: Social media, a website, or local markets.

DAY 13
RESEARCH FREE OR LOW-COST MARKETING STRATEGIES

ACTION!

LOOK UP THREE MARKETING IDEAS.

Example: Maybe social media, flyers, or word-of-mouth advertising.

DAY 14
TRACK YOUR PERSONAL SPENDING & FIND ONE WAY TO SAVE

ACTION!

LOOK AT HOW YOU'VE SPENT MONEY RECENTLY. IS THERE ONE THING YOU CAN CUT BACK ON TO SAVE FOR YOUR BUSINESS?

Example: If you skip buying a $5 USD snack every day for a month (about 30 days), you'll save around $150 USD for your business.

WEEK 3:
TAKING ACTION & BUILDING HABITS

This week is all about taking small but meaningful steps toward launching your business. You've spent time learning and planning—now it's time to apply what you've learned!

DAY 15
START SETTING ASIDE MONEY FOR YOUR BUSINESS

ACTION!

DECIDE HOW MUCH YOU CAN SET ASIDE EACH WEEK (EVEN IF IT'S $5 OR $10). PUT THIS MONEY IN A SAFE PLACE—A SAVINGS ACCOUNT, A SEPARATE JAR, OR EVEN A FINANCIAL APP.

Example: If you want to sell handmade jewelry, saving just $20 could buy the materials to make your first few products.

DAY 16
CREATE A SIMPLE LOGO OR BRAND STYLE (COLORS, THEME)

ACTION!

CHOOSE: 1. A BRAND COLOR SCHEME (3 MAIN COLORS). 2. A SIMPLE LOGO (YOU CAN DESIGN ONE ON CANVA FOR FREE). 3. A BUSINESS NAME.

Example: If you tutor kids in math, your brand colors might be blue & white (for a clean, professional look), and your logo could be your initials in a fun font.

DAY 17

WRITE A 3-4 SENTENCE PITCH ABOUT YOUR BUSINESS

ACTION!

WRITE A SHORT PITCH USING THIS FORMAT: 1. WHAT DO YOU DO? 2. WHO DO YOU HELP? 3. WHAT MAKES YOU UNIQUE?

Example: "I create personalized gift baskets for birthdays and special occasions. My designs are custom-made based on your budget and preferences. I make it easy to find the perfect, thoughtful gift without the hassle!"

DAY 18
SET UP A SOCIAL MEDIA PAGE OR TELL FAMILY AND FRIENDS

ACTION!

IF YOU'RE COMFORTABLE, CREATE AN INSTAGRAM, FACEBOOK, OR TIKTOK PAGE FOR YOUR BUSINESS. IF NOT, START BY TELLING 5 PEOPLE (FRIENDS, FAMILY, TEACHERS, NEIGHBORS).

Example: If you're selling custom t-shirts, posting pictures on Instagram or WhatsApp status can attract buyers.

DAY 19
IDENTIFY ONE PERSON WHO CAN MENTOR OR SUPPORT YOU

ACTION!

THINK OF ONE PERSON WHO HAS EXPERIENCE IN BUSINESS OR FINANCE. ASK THEM ONE QUESTION (E.G., "WHAT'S ONE PIECE OF ADVICE YOU WISH YOU KNEW BEFORE STARTING?").

Example: A teacher, family member, or entrepreneur you admire can be a great mentor.

DAY 20

RESEARCH 3 WAYS TO INCREASE YOUR INCOME (SIDE HUSTLES, SELLING SKILLS, ETC.)

ACTION!

RESEARCH AT LEAST THREE INCOME OPPORTUNITIES: SELLING A PRODUCT (E.G., HANDMADE ITEMS). OFFERING A SERVICE (E.G., TUTORING, GRAPHIC DESIGN). ONLINE INCOME (E.G., CONTENT CREATION).

Example: If you're good at writing, you could start a blog or offer freelance writing services.

DAY 21
REFLECT ON WHAT YOU'VE LEARNED ABOUT SAVING, SPENDING, AND EARNING

ACTION!

WRITE DOWN: 1. ONE THING YOU'VE DONE WELL. 2. ONE THING YOU WANT TO IMPROVE. 3. ONE FINANCIAL GOAL FOR THE NEXT MONTH.

Example: "I've been great at saving, but I need to be more consistent with marketing my business. Next month, I want to earn my first $100."

WEEK 4:
LAUNCHING & GROWING

This week, it's time to take action and put your business into the real world!

DAY 22
MAKE YOUR FIRST PRODUCT, SERVICE, OR CONTENT POST

IF YOU SELL PRODUCTS MAKE 1-3 ITEMS AND TAKE PHOTOS. IF YOU OFFER A SERVICE ANNOUNCE IT ON SOCIAL MEDIA OR TO FRIENDS. IF YOU'RE BUILDING AN ONLINE BRAND POST YOUR FIRST PIECE OF CONTENT.

Example: If you're a digital artist, post a sample of your work with a caption explaining your service.

DAY 23
PRACTICE EXPLAINING YOUR BUSINESS TO SOMEONE

ACTION!

FIND A FRIEND, TEACHER, OR PARENT AND EXPLAIN YOUR BUSINESS IDEA TO THEM IN UNDER 1 MINUTE. ASK FOR FEEDBACK—DO THEY UNDERSTAND IT? WHAT QUESTIONS DO THEY HAVE?

Example: If you design logos, practice saying: "I create unique logos for small businesses to help them stand out online."

DAY 24

SET A GOAL FOR HOW MANY CUSTOMERS OR SALES YOU WANT IN THE NEXT MONTH

ACTION!

CHOOSE A REALISTIC TARGET (E.G., "I WANT 5 CUSTOMERS THIS MONTH."). WRITE DOWN ONE ACTION STEP PER WEEK TO HELP REACH THAT GOAL.

Example: If you sell baked goods, your goal might be: "Sell 10 cupcakes per week." To achieve this, you could:

1. Post on social media every 3 days.
2. Offer a special discount to first-time buyers.
3. Ask friends & family to spread the word.

DAY 25

CREATE A SIMPLE BUDGET FOR YOUR BUSINESS EARNINGS

WRITE DOWN HOW MUCH YOU EARNED THIS MONTH. LIST YOUR EXPENSES (SUPPLIES, TOOLS, ADVERTISING). CALCULATE YOUR PROFIT: EARNINGS – EXPENSES = PROFIT. DECIDE HOW TO USE YOUR PROFIT (SAVE, REINVEST, PAY YOURSELF).

Example: Create a table/list with the headings: Amount Earned, Expenses, Profit, Save/Reinvest/Pay Yourself.

DAY 26
IDENTIFY ONE FINANCIAL MISTAKE TO AVOID

WRITE DOWN ONE FINANCIAL MISTAKE YOU'LL AVOID AND HOW YOU'LL PREVENT IT!

Example: Think of one common financial mistake that could hurt your business:

- Spending too much before making a profit
- Not tracking where your money goes
- Under-pricing products/services

DAY 27
START TRACKING HOW MUCH YOU EARN & SPEND

ACTION!

KNOWING YOUR NUMBERS = BUSINESS SUCCESS! KEEPING TRACK OF YOUR INCOME AND EXPENSES HELPS YOU SEE IF YOUR BUSINESS IS GROWING. WRITE DOWN EVERYTHING YOU EARN AND SPEND THIS WEEK. USE A NOTEBOOK, PHONE APP, OR THE BUDGET WORKSHEET FROM DAY 25.

Example: If you earned $50 from selling bracelets and spent $20 on supplies, write it down to track your profit.

____

____

____

____

____

DAY 28
FIND ONE WAY TO IMPROVE YOUR PRODUCT OR SERVICE

ACTION!

GOOD BUSINESSES ALWAYS IMPROVE! LOOK AT YOUR BUSINESS AND ASK: CAN I MAKE MY PRODUCT/SERVICE BETTER? CAN I OFFER BETTER CUSTOMER SERVICE? CAN I REACH MORE PEOPLE WITH MY MARKETING?

Example: "I can improve my lip gloss business by adding a thank-you card to each order to make customers feel appreciated."

DAY 29
WRITE DOWN WHAT WORKED, WHAT DIDN'T, & WHAT YOU'LL DO NEXT

TAKE TIME TO ANSWER THESE THREE QUESTIONS:

- **WHAT WORKED WELL IN MY BUSINESS THIS MONTH?**
- **WHAT CHALLENGES DID I FACE?**
- **WHAT WILL I DO DIFFERENTLY NEXT MONTH?**

Example: What worked? Promoting my business on Instagram etc. This reflection helps you learn from experience and plan for success.

DAY 30

CELEBRATE YOUR PROGRESS!

KEEP BUILDING YOUR FUTURE

YOU DID IT! NOW WHAT? LOOK BACK AT DAY 1—HOW MUCH HAVE YOU LEARNED? WHAT IS YOUR NEXT BIG GOAL? WRITE DOWN ONE ACTION STEP TO KEEP YOUR BUSINESS GROWING!

Example: Next big goal: design and launch website.

FINAL RECAP

FINAL RECAP

WHAT YOU'VE ACCOMPLISHED IN 30 DAYS:

- Identified your skills, talents & business ideas
- Created a simple business plan
- Set financial goals & tracked earnings

- Learned smart money habits & budgeting
- Started (or planned) your first business!

The Future Millionaire Mindset is just beginning—keep going!

BONUS TIP: HOW TO STAY CONSISTENT & KEEP GROWING

Success is a journey, not a one-time event!

Now that you've completed the 30-Day Financial Challenge, your next step is to stay consistent and keep improving.

Here are three things you can do every month to continue growing:

- **Set a New Goal:** Decide what you want to achieve next—more sales, better marketing, or a new product/service.
- **Track Your Progress:** Keep monitoring your income, expenses, and profits. The more you track, the more you'll understand your business.
- **Keep Learning:** Read books, watch videos, or find a mentor. The best entrepreneurs never stop learning!

LEVELING UP

MAKING YOUR BUSINESS OFFICIAL

LEVELING UP: MAKING YOUR BUSINESS OFFICIAL

BUSINESS REGISTRATION & STRUCTURE

Many countries require business registration before you can officially operate. Registering your business offers legal protection, enhances your credibility, and opens up financial opportunities, like the ability to open a business bank account or qualify for grants and loans.

TYPES OF BUSINESS REGISTRATION:

- **Sole Trader** – You own and run the business alone. This is the simplest and most common type of business structure.

- **Partnership** – You share the business with one or more people, and all partners contribute to decision-making and profits.

- **Limited Liability Company (LLC)** – A more formal business structure that separates personal assets from business liabilities, protecting you if the business runs into debt or legal issues.

WHAT SHOULD YOU DO?

- Research your country's business registration rules. Some places allow small-scale teen businesses to operate without immediate registration, while others require it before you start.
- If you're earning money consistently, talk to a parent or mentor about registration. They can guide you on legal requirements, taxes, and business structure.
- Learn about taxes – In most places, businesses must pay taxes once they start making a profit. Understanding this early will help you avoid legal issues later.

Even if you're just starting, knowing these rules early will help you grow your business the right way!

EXTRAS

TOOLS FOR YOUR FUTURE MILLIONAIRE JOURNEY

10 BUSINESS IDEAS FOR TEEN ENTREPRENEURS

Here are 10 business ideas for teens that are realistic, profitable, and easy to start:

1. TUTORING SERVICES

If you're good at math, science, or languages, offer tutoring services to younger students or peers who need help.

2. SOCIAL MEDIA MANAGEMENT

Many small businesses struggle with social media. If you know how to create engaging posts and grow followers, offer this service.

3. GRAPHIC DESIGN & DIGITAL ART

Teens with an eye for design can create logos, flyers, or social media graphics using free tools like Canva.

4. SELLING HANDMADE PRODUCTS

Make and sell jewelry, candles, custom T-shirts, or other crafts through platforms like Etsy or at local markets.

5. CAR WASH & DETAILING

Start a mobile car wash service in your neighborhood. Offer interior vacuuming and detailing for extra income.

6. PHOTOGRAPHY & CONTENT CREATION

If you have a good camera or smartphone, offer photography sessions for birthdays, graduations, or business products.

7. LAWN CARE & YARD WORK

Mowing lawns, pulling weeds, and planting flowers are simple services you can provide to neighbors.

8. BAKING & SNACK BUSINESS

Sell cookies, cupcakes, or healthy snacks at school, church, or local events.

9. PRINT-ON-DEMAND BUSINESS

Design and sell custom T-shirts, mugs, phone cases, or stickers using Printify or similar platforms. These services handle printing and shipping, so you don't need inventory—just great designs!

10. TECH HELP & WEBSITE BUILDING

If you're good with computers, offer basic tech support or build websites for small businesses.

PRAYERS FOR FINANCIAL WISDOM AND SUCCESS

SEEKING GOD'S GUIDANCE FOR FINANCIAL SUCCESS

Managing money isn't just about numbers—it's about having the right mindset, discipline, and faith to make wise financial decisions. Prayer invites God's wisdom, provision, and favor into our financial journey.

Whether you are saving, earning, giving, or spending, seeking His guidance will help you make choices that align with His purpose for your life.

These prayers will encourage and strengthen you as you develop healthy money habits, trust God with your resources, and walk in financial wisdom and success.

1. PRAYER FOR FINANCIAL WISDOM

Heavenly Father,

Thank You for giving me the ability to grow and learn about money. Help me to be wise in my financial decisions and to use my resources in ways that honor You. Teach me to be a good steward of what I have, whether little or much. Let me always seek Your guidance in managing money and growing wealth.

In Jesus' name, I pray. Amen.

2. PRAYER FOR SMART SPENDING & SELF-CONTROL

Dear Lord,

I ask for wisdom in how I spend my money. Sometimes, I am tempted to buy things I don't really need, and I ask for Your help in practicing self-control. Help me to prioritize what truly matters, to make wise spending choices, and to think about my future. Let me always be intentional with my finances.

In Jesus' name, I pray. Amen.

3. PRAYER FOR FINANCIAL GROWTH & GENEROSITY

Heavenly Father,

I thank You for the promise that You will provide for all my needs. Help me to not only build wealth but to use it wisely and generously. Teach me to give with a joyful heart and to always trust You as my Provider. I declare that I will be financially free, and I will use my wealth to make a positive impact in the world.

In Jesus' name, I pray. Amen.

GOAL TRACKER – YOUR FUTURE MILLIONAIRE GOALS

Instructions: Set your financial goals, write them down, and track your progress.

- **Financial Goal** – What do you want to achieve? *(Example: Save $500 USD)*
- **Why It's Important** – What's the purpose? *(Example: To start investing)*
- **Deadline** – By when do you want to achieve it? *(Example: 6 months)*
- **Progress** – How close are you? *(Example: 50% completed)*

FINANCIAL GOAL	WHY IT'S IMPORTANT	DEADLINE	PROGRESS

FINANCIAL GOAL	WHY IT'S IMPORTANT	DEADLINE	PROGRESS

BUDGET LIST – PLANNING YOUR MONEY WISELY

Instructions: Write down your expected income and expenses to create a simple budget.

- **Date** – Write the date you are budgeting for. (weekly, monthly)
- **Income** – How much money do you have coming in? (Allowances, side hustles, part-time work, gifts, etc.)
- **Expenses** – What are your expected costs? (School supplies, lunch money, phone bill, savings, giving, etc.)
- **Amount Left** – Subtract expenses from income to see what's left.
- **Adjustments** – Do you need to reduce spending or increase savings?

DATE	INCOME	EXPENSES	AMOUNT LEFT	ADJUSTMENTS

DATE	INCOME	EXPENSES	AMOUNT LEFT	ADJUSTMENTS

NEEDS & WANTS LIST – MAKING SMART SPENDING CHOICES

Instructions: Before spending, classify if it's a need (something essential) or a want (something you can live without).

- **Needs:** Things that are absolutely necessary *(food, transportation, school fees, savings).*
- **Wants:** Things that are nice to have but not urgent *(designer clothes, fast food, gaming subscriptions).*
- **Decision:** After listing your wants, ask yourself, *"Can I delay this and use my money for something more important?"*

NEEDS	WANTS	DECISION TO DELAY YES/NO

NEEDS	WANTS	DECISION TO DELAY YES/NO

DAILY SPENDING TRACKER – WHAT IS A NEED VS. WANT?

Instructions: Keep track of where your money goes each day to identify spending patterns.

- **Date** – When did you spend?
- **Item Purchased** – What did you buy?
- **Cost** – How much did it cost?
- **Need or Want?** – Classify if it was a need or want.
- **Could I Have Avoided It?** – Reflect on whether it was a necessary expense.

DATE	ITEM PURCHASED	COST	NEED OR WANT?	COULD I HAVE AVOIDED IT?

DATE	ITEM PURCHASED	COST	NEED OR WANT?	COULD I HAVE AVOIDED IT?

SAVINGS TRACKER – WATCH YOUR MONEY GROW

Instructions: Track your savings over time to see your progress toward your goals.

- **Date** – When did you save?
- **Amount Saved** – How much did you put aside?
- **Total Savings So Far** – Your growing balance.
- **Goal Amount** – What are you saving toward?
- **Remaining to Goal** – How much more do you need?

DATE	AMOUNT SAVED	TOTAL SAVINGS SO FAR	GOAL AMOUNT	REMAINING TO GOAL

DATE	AMOUNT SAVED	TOTAL SAVINGS SO FAR	GOAL AMOUNT	REMAINING TO GOAL

MOTIVATIONAL MESSAGE: YOUR FUTURE MILLIONAIRE MINDSET STARTS NOW!

You don't have to wait to be successful—you can start building your future today!

You now have the mindset, skills, and plan to take control of your financial future. No matter your age, background, or resources, you have everything you need to succeed.

Every dollar you save, every business move you make, and every smart decision brings you one step closer to financial freedom.

Believe in yourself. Stay consistent. Keep pushing forward.

Your journey to financial success has already begun—so keep going, keep growing, and never stop believing in your potential!

ANSWER KEY TO QUIZZES

CH. 1	CH. 2	CH. 3	CH. 4	CH. 5	CH. 6
1. B	1. B	1. C	1. C	1. C	1. B
2. C	2. B	2. C	2. C	2. C	2. A
3. B	3. B	3. B	3. C	3. D	3. C
4. B	4. B	4. B	4. C	4. C	4. D
5. B	5. C	5. C	5. B	5. C	5. C
6. C	6. C	6. C	6. C	6. B	6. C
7. A	7. C	7. B	7. C	7. B	7. C
8. C	8. B	8. C	8. B	8. C	8. A
9. C	9. B	9. B	9. A	9. C	9. D
10. C	10. D	10. C	10. C	10. C	10. C

CH. 7	CH. 8	CH. 9
1. C	1. C	1. C
2. C	2. A	2. C
3. B	3. B	3. B
4. B	4. B	4. A
5. B	5. D	5. D
6. C	6. B	6. B
7. B	7. B	7. C
8. B	8. C	8. C
9. C	9. C	9. B
10. C	10. B	10. C

GLOSSARY

FINANCIAL & BUSINESS TERMS

GLOSSARY OF FINANCIAL & BUSINESS TERMS

A

- **Account Balance** – The amount of money in a bank account at a given time.
- **Accounting** – The process of recording, analyzing, and managing financial transactions.
- **Accounts Payable (AP)** – Money a business owes to suppliers or creditors for goods and services received.
- **Accounts Receivable (AR)** – Money that customers owe a business for products or services provided.
- **Amortization** – The process of gradually paying off a debt in fixed payments over time.
- **Annual Percentage Rate (APR)** – The cost of borrowing money, expressed as a yearly percentage, including interest and fees.
- **Assets** – Anything valuable that a person or business owns, such as cash, property, or investments.
- **Audit** – A detailed examination of financial records to ensure accuracy and compliance with laws.
- **Automation** – Using technology to complete tasks without human involvement, often used in business and finance to save time and money.

B

- **Balance Sheet** – A financial statement that shows a company's assets, liabilities, and equity at a specific point in time.
- **Bankruptcy** – A legal process where a person or business cannot pay their debts and seeks relief from creditors.
- **Board of Directors** – A group of people elected to oversee the management of a company and make important business decisions.
- **Bond** – A type of investment where you lend money to a company or government, and they agree to pay it back with interest over time.
- **Bookkeeping** – The process of recording financial transactions in a business.
- **Budget** – A plan for how money will be earned, saved, and spent over a period of time.
- **Business Model** – A company's plan for making money and operating successfully.

C

- **Capital** – Money or assets that a business uses to start and grow.
- **Cash Flow** – The movement of money in and out of a business or personal finances.

- **CEO (Chief Executive Officer)** – The highest-ranking person in a company, responsible for making major decisions and leading the business.
- **CFO (Chief Financial Officer)** – The executive responsible for managing a company's finances.
- **Collateral** – Something of value, like property or a car, that is offered as security for a loan.
- **Compound Interest** – Interest that is earned not just on the initial amount of money but also on the interest that has already been added.
- **Consumer** – A person who buys goods or services.
- **Corporation** – A type of business that is legally separate from its owners and can raise money by selling shares (stock).
- **Credit** – The ability to borrow money now and pay it back later.
- **Credit Score** – A number that represents how well someone manages borrowed money and debts.
- **Cryptocurrency** – A digital form of money that operates on a decentralized system (e.g., Bitcoin, Ethereum).

D

- **Debt** – Money that is borrowed and must be paid back.
- **Depreciation** – The decrease in value of an asset over time, such as a car losing value as it ages.
- **Dividend** – A portion of a company's profits that is paid to shareholders.
- **Down Payment** – A part of the total price paid upfront when buying something expensive, like a house or car.

- **Due Diligence** – Research and investigation done before making a financial or business decision.

E

- **Earnings** – Money that a person or business makes.
- **Economy** – The system of how money, goods, and services are produced, bought, and sold in a country or the world.
- **Entrepreneur** – A person who starts and runs their own business.
- **Equity** – The value of ownership in something, like a business or property.
- **Expenses** – The money spent on goods and services, such as rent, salaries, and supplies.

F

- **Financial Freedom** – Having enough money to cover expenses and live comfortably without worrying about money.
- **Financial Literacy** – The ability to understand and manage money effectively.
- **Foreclosure** – When a bank takes back property, such as a house, because the owner couldn't pay the loan.
- **Franchise** – A type of business where an individual buys the rights to use a well-known company's brand and business model.

G

- **Gross Profit** – The money a business makes after subtracting the cost of producing goods or services but before deducting other expenses like rent, salaries, and taxes.
- **Guarantor** – A person who agrees to pay back a loan if the borrower fails to do so.

H

- **Human Resources (HR)** – The department in a company that manages employees, hiring, and workplace policies.

I

- **Income** – Money received from work, investments, or business activities.
- **Inflation** – The increase in prices over time, making goods and services more expensive.
- **Interest** – The cost of borrowing money or the money earned on savings and investments.
- **Investing** – Putting money into something, like stocks or real estate, with the hope of making a profit.

J

- **Joint Venture** – A business partnership where two or more parties work together on a specific project.

K

- **KPI (Key Performance Indicator)** – A measure used to track a company's success in achieving its goals.

L

- **Liabilities** – Debts or obligations that a person or business owes.
- **Limited Liability Company (LLC)** – A type of business structure that protects owners from personal responsibility for business debts.
- **Liquidity** – How easily something can be turned into cash without losing value.
- **Loan** – Money borrowed that must be paid back, usually with interest.

M

- **Marketing** – The process of promoting and selling products or services.
- **Monopoly** – When one company has complete control over a product or service, eliminating competition.

N

- **Net Profit** – The money a business actually keeps as profit after subtracting all expenses, including rent, wages, utilities, and taxes.

O

- **Offering** – A voluntary gift of money, resources, or time given to a church or charity, in addition to tithes, as an act of generosity and worship.
- **Overdraft** – When more money is withdrawn from a bank account than is available, creating a negative balance.

P

- **Partnership** – A business owned by two or more people who share profits and responsibilities.
- **Passive Income** – Money earned with little to no effort, such as from investments or rental properties.
- **Profit** – The money a business makes after subtracting expenses.

Q

- **Quarterly Earnings** – A company's financial results reported every three months.

R

- **Revenue** – The total money a business earns before expenses are deducted.
- **ROI (Return on Investment)** – A measure of how much money is gained or lost from an investment.

S

- **Savings** – Money set aside for future use.

- **Sole Proprietorship** – A business owned and run by one person.
- **Stock** – A share of ownership in a company.

T

- **Taxes** – Money paid to the government to fund public services.
- **Tithes** – A portion of a person's income, typically 10%, given to a church or religious organization as an act of faith and obedience to God. Tithing is a biblical principle where believers give back to God as a way of honoring Him and supporting the church's work.
- **Trade** – The buying and selling of goods and services.

U

- **Unsecured Loan** – A loan given without requiring collateral, based on trust and creditworthiness.

V

- **Venture Capital** – Money provided to startups and new businesses by investors looking for high returns.

W

- **Wealth** – The total value of everything a person owns, including money, property, and investments.
- **Wage** – Payment for work, usually based on hours worked.

Y

- **Yield** – The earnings generated from an investment, usually expressed as a percentage.

AUTHOR'S NOTE & SOURCES

AUTHOR'S NOTE

The Future Millionaire Mindset was written with a deep passion for equipping young people with financial wisdom that can change their future. As someone who has experienced both the challenges and opportunities that come with money, I believe that financial literacy is one of the most powerful tools for success.

This book is not just about money—**it's about mindset, discipline, and faith.** My goal is to help you develop smart financial habits early so that you can avoid common pitfalls and build a future of financial freedom and purpose.

SOURCES

The insights in this book are drawn from:

- Certificate in Personal Finance.
- Personal experience as an entrepreneur.
- Business coaching.
- Research-based financial principles from reputable sources in financial education.

- Biblical principles on stewardship, wealth-building, and generosity.
- Lessons from successful entrepreneurs and financial leaders.

This book is a practical guide, and while the principles are sound, I encourage readers to continue learning, seek professional financial advice when needed, and apply these strategies in ways that best suit their unique financial journey.

ABOUT THE AUTHOR

Cheleta Buddo-Gayle is a wife, mother, Christian author, entrepreneur, and speaker committed to empowering adults and youth to break free from financial struggles and step into financial freedom and purpose. She believes that faith, discipline, and financial literacy are the keys to lasting success.

From an early age, Cheleta embraced the entrepreneurial mindset, starting her first business at just nine years old. Through her journey of business, setbacks, and financial growth, she developed a passion for helping others manage money wisely, make smart investments, and create wealth with intention.

As the CEO and Founder of Christ RepresentHER, Cheleta is dedicated to helping individuals heal, grow, and thrive through faith-driven education and mentorship. She is also a devoted wife and mother who actively teaches financial principles to her children, ensuring they develop the habits of wise money management, financial responsibility, and wealth-building from an early age.

Cheleta is the author of **Breaking Procrastination and the Spirit of Poverty** and several other transformational books designed to inspire action, financial growth, and personal development.

Through **The Future Millionaire Mindset,** she equips readers with practical financial tools and biblical principles of stewardship, helping them build wealth, avoid financial pitfalls, and confidently pursue their God-given purpose.

For inquiries, bulk orders, or speaking engagements, you can connect with Cheleta Buddo-Gayle via email at:
christrepresenther@gmail.com

www.ingramcontent.com/pod-product-compliance
Lightning Source LLC
Chambersburg PA
CBHW041302210926
51847CB00010B/107
9789769747678